John Fenton has helped many comj
performance by applying the principle
what some of his clients have to say at

"It really worked. This has been the best selling year in our history. New orders are more than 40% up on last year and success stories spread across every product line and every sales area."
Philip Bullus
Bournes Electronics Limited

"We have actually managed to increase our business over the past two years by 25% per year, a lot of which could not have been achieved had we not used the information and ideas given by you."
Dick Goodall
Aquatech Marketing Limited

"Excellent, stimulating, practical, true, feasible, vital."
A. E. Judd
Industrial Division - Crane Heatex

"Impressive and important. Can't fail to improve results."
Peter McArthur
Link 51

"Really worthwhile and absolutely worth every penny."
Vincent Brinkhof
Standard & Poor's

"So many simple ideas that can greatly increase our business."
Angus Beston
Protim Solignum Ltd

"Excellent. It has provided many new ideas."
Roger Chadwick
Labeltech Ltd

"Your input on how we quote meant that we improved turnover by 20% on last year and maintained our margin."
Eddie Mander
CGS Catering Equipment

"Your CFO List has given us an edge not one of our 400 competitors can beat."
Ian Garner
The Hobart Manufacturing Co. Ltd

"Your proposal folder, testimonials and CFO List will give us another £10 million sales over the next three years, for the same number of quotations."
Chris Smith
Southern Print (Web Offset) Ltd

"So far, I've had 100% success closing proposals that I've produced since you gave us the know-how."
Martin Sewell
Marketing Initiatives Ltd

"Our Quotes to Order Ratio has improved from 25 to 1 down to 4.5 to 1 since you gave us the treatment. That's 5.5 times as many Orders from the same number of Quotations."
Ernie Johnson
GKN Sankey Limited

VISION STATEMENT

The Profession of Selling

It is a glaring glimpse of the obvious to say that no amount of production is the slightest value unless the products are sold for cash.

Selling is the very crux of any commercial or industrial enterprise.

It therefore stands to reason that, as a nation which depends so heavily on selling our products abroad, it is very much in the national interest that the highest standards and the most advanced techniques in salesmanship should be encouraged.

HRH Prince Philip

Duke of Edinburgh KG, KT

MASTER CLOSER

For a complete list of Management Books 2000 titles
visit our web-site on http://www.mb2000.com

MASTER CLOSER

John Fenton

2000

First published in 2009 by Management Books 2000 Ltd
Forge House, Limes Road
Kemble, Cirencester
Gloucestershire, GL7 6AD, UK
Tel: 0044 (0) 1285 771441
Fax: 0044 (0) 1285 771055
Email: info@mb2000.com
Web: www.mb2000.com

British Library Cataloguing in Publication Data is available

ISBN 9781852525750

MASTER CLOSER...

IF YOU AND YOUR SALESPEOPLE COULD EARN THIS ACCOLADE, WHERE WOULD YOUR SALES BE THIS TIME NEXT YEAR?

'If you don't close, you're working for the competition!'
Alfred Tack

'Almost every buying decision has some negative aspects from the customer's point of view, and these have to be overcome through the use of an appropriate closing technique.'
Heinz M. Goldmann

'You haven't done your job if you quit without asking for the order at least five times.'
J. Douglas Edwards

'In selling, our income and achievement depends almost entirely on our ability to close.'
Robin Fielder

Contents

Preface 15
    The Pressure of Closing.. *16*
    The Ethics of Closing *16*
    The One-In-Five Survey.. *17*
    The 8/73 Survey... *17*
    The Best Closers.. *19*
    Excuses... *20*
    Closing with your Quotation....................................... *21*

About the Author... 23

1 Expectations.. 25
    The Medical Statistics *25*
    The 8/73 Analysis.. *25*
    Determining sales policy... *26*
    Your Drive and Energy system..................................... *33*

2 Opening Time 37
    Using the five words that really turn customers on *38*
    Questioning Techniques.. *44*
    Ice Breakers *46*
    Other ways of making appointments *47*

3 Developing the Sale 49
    The Feel Good Factor... *49*
    What you can do to make the customers feel good about YOU.. *50*
    What you can do to make the Customers feel good about
        THE SOLUTION.. *54*
    What you can do to make the Customers feel good about
        THE PRICE *55*

What can we do to make the customers feel good about
THE SUPPLIER *60*

4 Establishing Customer Objectives **61**

5 Preparing a Proposal **73**
1. The Customer's Objectives *73*
2. Your Recommendations *73*
3. Summary of Additional Benefits *74*
4. Financial Justification *74*
5. Your Guarantees and After-Sales Service *75*

6 Negotiating **77**
Negotiating on the Merits *77*

7 Closing Time **81**
Popular closing techniques *83*
Salesmen's favourite closes *93*
Two additional closing tools *94*
Starting with a Close *95*

8 Overcoming Price-Conditioning **97**
Never Knock the Competition *98*
Justify the Difference *99*
The Right Way to Close on a Discount *99*
The Added-Value Close *100*
The John Ruskin Close *100*
Don't State It, Sell It *101*

9 Closing with a Clipboard **103**
The Order Form Close *103*
The Criteria for Ordering Close *104*
The Ben Franklin Balance Sheet *105*
The Options Lost Close *106*
The Wedding-Cake Close *106*
The Diary Close *107*

Contents

Signing-Up Techniques *108*
X Marks the Spot *108*
The Objectives Checklist *109*

10 Closing over the Telephone **111**
The Twin-Track Approach *112*
Trial Closing *114*
Selling Across *115*
Selling Up *115*
Closing on a Complaint *116*
'Following Up Quotation' Closes *117*
Exploding the Myth *118*

11 Classic Closes **119**
When Is an Order Really Lost *119*
The 'Price Is Higher' Close *120*
The 'Phone the Boss' Close *120*
The Coffee Percolator Close *121*
Public Closes *122*
The Real Close *123*
The Clive Holmes Cocktail Party Close *123*
The Victor Hugo Close *124*
The Audiocassette Close *124*
Closing a Closed Tender *125*
The 'We've a Van in Your Area Tomorrow' Close *126*

12 Closing a Board of Directors **129**
The Behavioural Mix *130*
How to Control the Meeting *133*
Flip Charts *134*
The Quality Close *135*
Closing with Figures *135*
The Big Gun Close *136*
Using the Boardroom Mole *137*
The Long Walk Close *137*

13 Making Sure the Customer is *Ready* to be Closed............ **139**
Don't Make Assumptions *140*
Getting to the Right Person.. *141*
Ensure Complete Understanding *144*
The Japanese Way... *144*
Aim to Achieve a Win-Win Situation..................................... *146*
Watch for the 'Ready' Signals.. *146*
When you ask for the close.. *153*

14 Becoming a Master Closer.. **155**
The Inner Game *156*
Parking Places A'Plenty *157*
Our conscious mind *158*
Our subconscious mind.. *159*
Our self-image... *159*
Self-Talk *161*

15 Moving On to the Next Sale... **163**
Getting Referrals... *163*
Using your mobile phone *163*
Converting your card-carrying troops................................... *165*
How to end every call.. *166*
The You're Pulling My Leg Close... *169*

16 Determining Your Selling Style... **171**

Index **175**

Preface

In every survey ever conducted, asking sales managers what skill they would most like to increase in their sales people, CLOSING has always emerged as the clear winner.

Can you succeed in selling without being a good *Closer*? The short answer is *NO, YOU CAN'T*.

The long answer begins with why the hell such a dumb question was asked in the first place. And the answer to that is because there are so many salespeople out there who can't *Close*, who don't *Close*, who forget to *Close*, who are frightened of *Closing*, who are terrified of being turned down and won't put themselves in the turndown-risk situation, who are so negative they expect a 'No' before they even start selling – *'You don't want any more Widgets this month, J suppose, do you?'*

Master Closer is for all those naive salespeople who feel *Closing* is unreal, not for them, not necessary in their business, unethical, high pressure and too complicated.

Master Closer is also for all those professional salespeople who have already recognised that *Closing* is for real, forever and very necessary, and want to be even better at it than they are now – and richer!

Closing is not high pressure. *Closing* is not unethical. If you are being paid to sell and you don't *Close*, you are taking money under false pretences. That's stealing! That's fraud! If you are being paid to sell and you don't *Close*, you are working for the competition. That's treason!

In this introduction I am going to convince you, with the aid of logic, facts and statistics, survey results and PROOF, that you cannot survive in Selling without being an effective *Closer*.

The Pressure of Closing

Let's sympathise with all those thousands of salespeople who think that when you use a *Closing* technique, you are applying pressure to the customer.

What is a *Closing* technique? It is anything you can ethically do or say that gets you closer to the decision to buy. For example:

> '*Are you happy with everything?*' *(pause, two, three.)*
> Customer: '*Er, yyyess, I think so.*'
> '*Fine. Can we go ahead, then?*' (Shut up.)

This must be the simplest pair of questions you can ask a customer at the end of a good sales presentation. All doubts are clarified.

That's why we said, 'Let's sympathise with all those thousands of salespeople ... because they haven't even gotten this bit right.

Where is the pressure? Think about it. Sure, the pressure is in the silence, but all the customer is doing during those few seconds of silence is mulling things over: '*Should I, shouldn't I? Seems OK. Solves our problem. Can't see any snags. Why not? OK, then.*' That's how the customer's mind is working.

So who's sweating? You, dummy. The pressure is on you, not the customer. It's unbearable. And after three seconds of silence you open your stupid fat mouth and ruin the customer's train of thought.

The Ethics of Closing

Professional salespeople don't beat up old ladies.

Professional salespeople don't put their foot in the door, seduce the customer's secretary, grab the customer's tie and tighten the knot until they say 'Yes', knock their competitors, keep selling after they've established that no need exists for their product or service, or after they've established that the customer cannot afford to buy.

And professional salespeople don't lie. They don't mislead or misrepresent. They don't exaggerate or give deliberately optimistic delivery dates. They don't promise future delights and rewards that they know will never exist. They don't oversell.

There are three lies that salespeople *can* tell. These are: *'It's my fault'*, *'You're right'* and *'It's been a pleasure to meet you'*.

The One-In-Five Survey

A comprehensive survey conducted by The Institute of Purchasing Management which covered all kinds of people who buy things – purchasing officers, production managers, directors and the whole range of specifiers – established beyond any doubt that:

> *Only one in five customers will ever volunteer an order. The other four out of five expect, on principle, the salesperson to ask for the order.*

If the salesperson doesn't ask, he or she goes away empty handed. Believe it. It's true.

So, statistically, those salespeople who never *Close*, who never ask for the order, don't even have a chance with 80 per cent of the market that *Master Closers* can benefit from.

Of course, you never know which of any five customers is the one who will volunteer an order. So, the only logical thing to do with this situation is:

> *Never Let A Potential Order Go Un-Asked For.*

The 8/73 Survey

International research conducted by John Fenton Stratagems plc into both salespeople and their customers is now known as the 8/73 Survey. The main research was conducted to find out how salespeople reacted to objections from their customers. An objection is a doubt in the customer's mind that is voiced: something they are not sure about, are worried about, are not clear about or don't like about the proposition.

Rarely indeed will a salesperson sail smoothly through a sales presentation, from the opening thirty seconds to the writing-up of the order, without encountering a single objection. Things are simply not that easy.

Objections are like hurdles in a race: you know they're going to be there, you know you've got to get over them, you know what direction you're running in and you know where the finishing tape is. Your only problem is physical. Can you get over all the hurdles and reach the finishing-tape before you run out of steam? The answer will be a measure of your fitness to sell the particular products or services that you have been given responsibility for. Many customers are not very forthcoming about voicing their doubts. They need to be encouraged. Otherwise they bottle them up and the salesperson, when **Closing Time** arrives, gets a *'No'* in response to the first attempt to ask for the order. And many salespeople, faced with this *'No'* mentally breathe a big sigh of relief and escape as fast as possible, convincing themselves that they've done the best they can.

Wrong, Wrong, Wrong!

Nine times out of ten 'No' wasn't a real 'No', it was the customer's way of saying, 'I'm not quite sure, yet.' And a 'No, not yet' is very, very different from, 'No, not ever', as you will learn in *Master Closer*.

Back to the 8/73 Survey. For the purpose of presenting the figures, all *'Nos'* are classified as *'No, not yets'*, that is, objections based on a doubt. Research on the reaction of salespeople to the objections they received from their customers revealed ...

> 44 per cent gave up after receiving the first objection.
> 22 per cent gave up after receiving the second objection.
> 16 per cent gave up after receiving the third objection.
> 10 per cent gave up after receiving the fourth objection.

So, 92 per cent gave up after four objections, leaving only 8 per cent of salespeople still selling. That's the 8 part of the 8/73 Survey.

The 73 part comes from the second half of the research which concentrated on the customers in order to establish the kind and the quantity of objections they voiced when faced with the salespeople they'd been dealing with.

The kinds of objections pinpointed are not relevant here, but the quantity is. The research established without any doubt that 73 per cent of customers voiced *five or more* objections before being sure enough to place an order.

In fact, the situation is significantly *worse* than this, because both the 92 per cent of salespeople who gave up and the 8 per cent still going after four objections are the salespeople who actually got as far as asking for the order *at least once*. The salespeople who don't close at all aren't even in the race.

The Best Closers

Now I'm going to hit you where it really hurts. Smack in your ego! Who are the best *Closers*? Who are the people who never give up, who never take no for an answer? Answer: children between the ages of six and nine.

Visualise a sunny morning in the park, just before lunch.

> *'Dad, can I have an ice cream?'*
> *'No, it's too near your lunchtime.'*
> *'Oh, go on Dad. Just a little one.'*
> *'No, I've told you.'*
> *'Oh, please Dad. I want one.'*
> *'No, that's enough.'*
> *Tears and fifty more decibels...*
> *'I wanna IIICE CREEEEEEAAM.'*
> *'Oh, for goodness sake. All right. But don't tell your mother.'*

Your kids never give up. Why is that? It's because before the age of nine their conditioning hasn't taken effect. Think about it. All through life, through your early childhood, through school, through early adulthood and your first taste of commerce ... ***whatever you wanted to do, someone, somewhere, always said No!***

We are all thoroughly conditioned to expect *'No'*. Is it therefore any wonder that it's always been so difficult getting to grips with **Closing** a sale?

Apart from taking note of techniques we are going to teach you so that you can become a *Master Closer*, all you have to do is change your normal in-built *'No'* expectation into a *'Yes'* expectation.

Then there are all the Excuses...

Excuses

Sales Managers... have you ever analysed the call reports you receive from your salespeople over, say, a six-month period, to pinpoint the kind of excuses they give for not coming away with an order? Note. 'excuses', not reasons!

Here are my own universal **Top Ten Excuses** for not *Closing*.

1. *The customer wants to think it over for a few days.*
2. *The customer wants to wait until the other quotations have been received.*
3. *The customer doesn't want to spend that kind of money.*
4. *The customer wants more discount than we can give them.*
5. *The customer wants to stick to their normal supplier.*
6. *The customer needs it by next week and we can't deliver for four weeks.*
7. *The customer doesn't think enough of their customers will buy it.*
8. *The customer feels it is too much trouble to change over.*
9. *The customer feels it is too complicated for their people.*
10. *The customer was too busy to listen properly.*

Any of these bring back memories of last week or last month? There are many ways to eliminate, or at least minimise these kinds of excuses for not *Closing*.

First let us dwell on three more things that will stop you getting the order, three that you will never in a million years see on any salesperson's call report. These are my **Top Three Reasons** (not excuses) for losing the order.

1. *I loused up the demonstration.*
2. *I got up the customer's nose by:*
    *   *Arriving twenty minutes late*
    *   *Not having the right spec sheet*
    *   *Smoking in the customer's office*
3. *Smelling like a brewery*

And the reason that eclipses all the other twelve rolled into one:

I DIDN'T ASK FOR THE ORDER.

Closing with your Quotation

Not just in the UK but worldwide, 98 per cent of ALL business-to-business businesses DO business with a Quotation.

Most of the business that is quoted for, especially the NEW business, throughout Industry and Commerce, is **LOST** – mainly because the Quotation fails to do the job it is supposed to do.

The Quotation format used by those 98 per cent of business-to business businesses was designed during the latter days of the Industrial Revolution: 150 years ago. It was designed as a legal document to protect suppliers being ripped off by unscrupulous customers in the biggest, strongest Sellers' Market the World has ever known. Often, the Quotation looks more like an invoice, is as user-friendly as an invoice and turns the customers *OFF* like an invoice.

Today – and well into the future – we face the strongest **BUYERS'** Market the World has ever known. Not the biggest, because the markets are steadily shrinking. There are far too many suppliers and far too few customers. Only those few suppliers who are selling at the lowest price can succeed in this highly competitive business environment – if they continue to stay with the current quotation format.

All the other suppliers – 95 per cent of the worldwide business-to-business businesses must *CHANGE* the way they quote for business if they want to survive and prosper.

They must learn how to produce Quotations which actually help them to *SELL THEIR HIGHER PRICE* – Quotations which turn customers who have traditionally bought on the basis of lowest price, into customers who see clearly the merits of buying on the basis of best value for money.

> *Every single one of these businesses could literally double the orders they win from the same number of quotations they submit – if they knew how!*

In *Master Closer* they'll find out *HOW!*

About the Author

John Fenton is probably Britain's best-known business Guru.

His selling, sales management and board level experience embraces hydraulics, materials handling equipment, machine tools, furniture manufacture, plastic extrusions, paper based systems, publishing, professional services and property development. He has trained salespeople and managers around the globe in hundreds of other businesses.

John Fenton was the man who declared 1983 'The Year for Selling'.

That year, with 25 massive sales shows and the first ever National Sales Convention at the Royal Albert Hall, he helped 47,000 British salespeople find their way out of that particular 'great recession'.

It was his white suit, worn on these shows, that earned him the accolade 'The Billy Graham of Selling'. Twenty-six years and twelve more National Sales Conventions on he is still best remembered for the white suited, evangelical, showbiz style he adopted to motivate his audiences during this period of his career.

Five of his best-selling books have vision statements by HRH Prince Philip, Duke of Edinburgh KG KT. In 1989 he sold his business interests for close to £10 Million and took a two-year 'don't compete' sabbatical during which he acquired a PhD in Applied Psychology, an MBA and a BCom in Marketing before launching John Fenton Stratagems plc.

His belief in what he does best can be summed up with the heading of his own foreword in his four 'Profession of Selling' books – 'SELLING IS THE MOST IMPORTANT JOB IN THE BUSINESS WORLD'.

John Fenton not only believes this, he has the personal charisma and enthusiasm to make his audiences and his delegates believe it. He talks to salesforces and business managers about WINNING;

about achieving outstanding results; about never taking second place to a competitor; about developing that all-important PMA; about creativity and being different and better than the rest.

1

Expectations

The Medical Statistics

- No-one has ever been struck by lightning for asking for the order
- Closing the sale has never caused a fatality
- It is one of the safest pastimes in the world

The 8/73 Analysis

As mentioned earlier, 44% of salespeople quit after the first objection; 22% quit after the second objection; 16% quit after the third objection; and 10% quit after the fourth – leaving just 8% still selling. And they have the 73% of buyers who give five or more objections all to themselves...

And remember that an objection does not indicate a lack of interest. Far from it – it is just an objection to saying YES and if the customer is still talking to you after four objections, they are interested...

In this chapter we will examine the attitudes required to become a successful **Master Closer**. Persistence is, of course, important. But you will also need to develop a consistently positive approach to all aspects of sales performance. The following exercises will help to focus your thinking on the way in which your attitudes and expectations can be enhanced to ensure optimum sales performance.

Determining sales policy

This is an individual exercise. There follow five pages with the headings:

PLANNING TIME
PROSPECTING
EXISTING CUSTOMERS
SALES INTERVIEWS
SELF APPRAISAL

Each section contains a series of statements relating to the topic concerned.

Take one topic at a time and decide which statement defines the approach to the topic that would be likely to result in the ***most profit*** for a company.

Then take the remaining statements and from these, chose the next most effective – and so on. Finally you will be left with the least effective approach.

Take each statement as a whole and form a reasonably rapid personal opinion. ***DO NOT*** note down what seems to happen in your own company. Select the approach which seems to you the best.

Record your results on each page in the 'Your Result' columns.

Complete each topic before moving to the next.

SECTION 1 – PLANNING TIME

A. I structure my activities well enough to achieve a good level of performance without too many problems. I always find that working to an orderly routine eases the pressures on me.

B. I plan my schedule well in advance and do my best to avoid deviating from it. By having my activities well organised I can use my selling time to maximum advantage.

C. I plan my work programme in advance but it has to be flexible. I must be available at my customers' disposal when they need me.

D. My customers contact me quite frequently and their requests keep me busy enough. Because of this I find little need to schedule my forward activities with much precision.

E. I put effort into planning my activities in terms of sales objectives. By doing this, I find that I can carry out my responsibilities and can minimise and control emergencies.

Your ranking

1(Best) ....

2 ....

3 ....

4 ....

5(Worst) ....

SECTION 2 – PROSPECTING FOR NEW CUSTOMERS

A. Prospecting is vital to company growth and I know how much new business I need. I see each customer as a good lead to new contacts and seek prospects in similar market categories.

B. I track down every prospect that comes to my attention. I push myself to make a specific number of new contacts each week on a cold canvassing basis if necessary.

C. When I have the time, I follow up on any enquiries which come my way, but most of my new business seems to come from my existing customers.

D. I ask the customers with whom I have a good relationship for their suggestions concerning new people to contact. I follow up any indication of positive interest.

E. I follow through on most leads that come in and create my own from lists and statistical documents. I increase my prospecting efforts whenever it appears I am falling behind.

Your ranking

1(Best)   ....

2   ....

3   ....

4   ....

5(Worst)   ....

SECTION 3 – LOOKING AFTER EXISTING CUSTOMERS

A. I ensure that my company provides top service at all times. By keeping in touch with the customer I try to anticipate their requirements. Continued satisfaction cements business relationships.

B. I act as a link between my company's internal organisation and the customer. Every customer is entitled to fair treatment.

C. I make regular visits to my customers and am happy when I can help them – particularly when this involves some service which is beyond their normal expectations.

D. Since I intend to sell them more, the customer must be made to feel that they are the boss. I keep constant pressure on my company to ensure that the customer's requirements are satisfied.

E. The business is out of my hands when it reaches the office. The customer will let me know whether they need anything else from us and I shall pass the message on to my office.

Your ranking

1(Best)   ....

2   ....

3   ....

4   ....

5(Worst)   ....

29

SECTION 4 – SALES INTERVIEWS

A. I describe the product to the prospect and, if it matches their needs, the sale is made. If they decide to buy I am ready to take their order, otherwise, I let them know where I can be reached.

B. The first essential is to be accepted as a person. I point out interesting features of my product, listen carefully to their reaction, and take my cue from the prospect. My customers would be antagonised by any suggestion of pressure tactics.

C. I start by establishing a relationship so that I can adapt my normal sales presentation accordingly. I emphasise reliability and never make claims which I cannot prove. A sale is often made through bargaining and compromise.

D. I aid the prospect to identify their needs, wants and problems considering both the practical and the emotional aspects. I summarise at the end and help them to a positive decision based on all the relevant factors.

E. My job is to get the product into the prospect's hands. I open with impact and focus their attention on the positive features. I try to convince them that a decision to buy will be both sound and rational.

Your ranking

1(Best)   ....

2   ....

3   ....

4   ....

5(Worst)   ....

SECTION 5 – SELF APPRAISAL

A. I improve my selling skills and increase my professional contribution by carefully analysing the causes of any failure, as well as the reasons for success.

B. Regular self-appraisal helps me to discover where I may be getting out of step and to rectify any problems before they get out of hand.

C. I am always aware of how others are reacting to me and I try to behave in a way that increases their acceptance of me. A good personality is essential in selling products and services.

D. I feel no real need to be continually reviewing my performance. The boss will tell me what I need to know and, if anything were to go wrong, 1 am sure 1 should hear about it soon enough.

E. I analyse the record of my sales results to make sure that I am keeping ahead. Some self appraisal of failures may be useful, but for me it is the diligent effort that improves performance.

Your ranking

1(Best)   ....

2   ....

3   ....

4   ....

5(Worst)   ....

RESULTS

When you have finished reading this book, check your answers again and see if you have changed any of your priorities. True Master Closers will tend to favour the stronger, more proactive approaches in all categories. Thus they would choose E as their favoured position in Section 1, A in Sections 2 and 3, E in Section 4, and A in Section 5. How did you compare?

Your Drive and Energy system

Drive and Energy are inseparable. One cannot function without the other. A good way to bring the two into line with your current sales expectations is to identify the two most negative influences on each and then work out specific ways to combat these influences. Try the following exercise:

YOUR DRIVE CAN BE DRAINED BY TWO THINGS:

1.   ....

How to counteract this:

    ....

    ....

    ....

    ....

2.   ....

How to counteract this:

    ....

    ....

    ....

    ....

YOUR ENERGY CAN BE DRAINED BY TWO THINGS:

1. ....

How to counteract this:

....

....

....

....

2. ....

How to counteract this:

....

....

....

....

These preliminary exercises should have helped you to focus on generating a more constructive, organised, proactive and above all POSITIVE approach to developing your sales techniques.

Now let us move on to the nitty-gritty – the specific techniques which will enable you to get your sales really motoring.

2

Opening Time

So, you have got your foot in the door... You're talking to your potential customer, and he asks:

'WHAT DO YOU WANT TO TALK TO ME ABOUT?'

Here's your answer:

Well, from the research we've been doing, I think we may be able to [and pick one or more of the following]

INCREASE   *your profits your sales*

IMPROVE   *your cash flow your buying power*

REDUCE   *your operating costs*
your scrap rates

SAVE   *your money*
you time

GAIN   *new contracts for you*
market share for you

Using the five words that really turn customers on

INCREASE
IMPROVE
REDUCE
SAVE
GAIN

Part 1

For each of the words or phrases listed below, select the key starter word (from the five listed above) that you think fits best. You can only choose one KSW for each line.

.... Ability to Expand
.... Accuracy
.... Boredom
.... Brand Awareness
.... Business
.... Buying Power
.... Cash Flow
.... Confidentiality
.... Choice
.... Costs
.... Credit Control
.... Customer Care
.... Customers
.... Data Security
.... Debtors
.... Delivery
.... Delivery Costs
.... Down Time
.... Efficiency
.... Effort
.... Energy

.... Errors
.... Experience
.... Finish (of Product)
.... Fuel Costs
.... Health
.... Image
.... Independence
.... Information
.... Knowledge
.... Labour Relations
.... Liability
.... Maintenance
.... Maintenance Costs
.... Market Share
.... Mobility
.... Money
.... New Contacts
.... New Contracts
.... New Customers
.... Output
.... Overheads
.... Packaging
.... Paperwork
.... Peace of Mind
.... Performance
.... Postage
.... Posture
.... Power
.... Prestige
.... Production
.... Profit
.... Public Relations
.... Quality
.... Quality of Life
.... Reject Rate
.... Reliability

.... Results
.... Risks
.... Running Costs
.... Safety
.... Salaries
.... Sales
.... Scrap
.... Security
.... Service
.... Shelf Life
.... Skills
.... Space
.... Speed of Information
.... Staff
.... Stock Levels
.... Stress
.... Support
.... Time
.... Travel
.... Trust
.... Turnover
.... Wear & Tear
.... Workforce Flexibility
.... Working Conditions

Part 2

Now select those lines which you can deliver for your customers –
i.e. the lines which you believe you can help your customers achieve
– and transfer them to the next page in the appropriate place.

When you do this, think about your specific customer and by how
much you will be able to INCREASE, IMPROVE, REDUCE, SAVE
or HELP them GAIN. Think PERCENTAGES.

Think the ACTUAL MONEY you will help them save or make.
BE BRAVE, THINK BIG.

THINK BIG
WRITE BIG
THINK MONEY
BIG MONEY

INCREASE   ....

....

....

....

IMPROVE   ....

....

. ...

....

REDUCE   ....

....

....

....

SAVE   ....

....

....

....

GAIN   ....

....

....

....

In case you had problems with Part 1, here is a breakdown of the possibilities, with a few new ones thrown in for good measure:

INCREASE

Advertising	Man Hours	Profit
Brand Awareness	Marketing Material	Quality of Life
Choice	Information Speed	Quality Standards
Credit Limits	Installations	Market Share
Customer Base	Knowledge	Mobility
Efficiency	Man Hours	Production
Image Awareness	Marketing Material	Profit
Information Speed	Market Share	Quality of Life
Installations	Mobility	Quality Standards
Knowledge	Production	

IMPROVE

Ability to Expand	Knowledge	Quality
Brand Awareness	Labour Relations	Reliability
Buying Power	Maintenance	Response Time
Cash Flow	Memory	Safety
Communication	Mobility	Security
Confidence	Morale	Skills
Credit Control	Performance	System
Delivery	Packaging	Team Spirit
Efficiency	Posture	Technical Awareness
Finish of Product	Procedures	Accuracy
Health	Product Display	Warranty
Image	Product Knowledge	Working Conditions
Independence	Product Range	Workforce Flexibility
Information	Public Relations	Working Conditions

REDUCE

Administration	Fuel Costs	Service
Back Orders	Gossip	Staff
Boredom	Labour	Stock Levels
Costs	Liability	Stress
Debtors	Maintenance Costs	Technical Problems
Down Time	Paperwork	Time
Errors	Range	Travel
False Alarms	Rejections	Waste
Damage	Risks	Wild Goose Chase
Delivery Costs	Running costs	
Delivery Times	Salaries	

SAVE

Effort	Packaging	Space
Energy	Paper	Time
Expenses	Postage	Trees
Face	Power	V.O.R.
Labour	Production Time	Wear & Tear
Money	Rush Jobs	Wasted Journeys

GAIN

Adhesion	Goals	Profitability
Business	Happiness	Protection
Cohesion	Hope	Public Awareness
Confidence	Information	Referrals
Confidentiality	Knowledge	Respect
Credibility	Loyalty	Simplicity
Customers	Market Share	Staff
Data Security	Mobility	Status
Data Security	Output	Steadiness
Experience	Positivity	Success
Faith	Prestige	Support
Flexibility	Profit	Trust

Questioning Techniques

Closed-ended questions

These should be used only when you want a commitment. They are hopeless for getting you information.

Examples:

> *'Are you happy with your present car?'*
> *'Can we go ahead, then?'*
> *'Do you want us to deliver?'*

Open-ended questions

These will get you the facts. They CANNOT be answered with 'YES' or 'NO'.
   Start with one of these words:

WHO, WHAT, WHY, HOW; WHEN, WHERE, WHICH?

Examples:

> *'How do you think your present car could be improved?'*
> *'What are you doing about this problem?'*
> *'Who else is involved in trying to find an economic solution?'*

Quality questions

A Quality question is one which gets you a Quality answer.

Example:

A police officer wouldn't ask 'How fast were you going?' If they did, they would likely get the response 'Not very fast!'
   They're trained to ask Quality questions, like, 'What do you estimate was the speed at which your vehicle was travelling on the day and at the time in question?'
   Now they are likely to get the response '68 to 70 miles an hour.'

'How thick was the fog?' 'Pretty thick!'

What can you do with that information? Not a lot.

'What do you estimate the visibility distance was at that time?'

'Oh, about the length of three double-decker buses. I know because I was stuck behind them for over an hour!'

A Quality question and a Quality answer. A quantified answer. Something you can do something with. Develop. Build on.

Positive and negative questions

'You don't need any more widgets this month I suppose?'

A negative question inviting a negative answer, 'No.'

'How many more widgets are you likely to need for the next three months, and when should we schedule deliveries?' Positive and much more likely to get you a positive response.

In a survey of thousands of shoppers asked the question 'Do you think it is okay to smoke whilst you are praying?' 87% said 'No'.

Then the survey changed the question for thousands more shoppers, to 'Do you think it is okay to pray whilst you are smoking?' 93% said 'Yes'.

Getting your Questions right needs constant practice. You also need to develop the art of LISTENING – to yourself as well as to what your customers say to you.

Ice Breakers

If you have trouble setting up the first meeting, try the following script:

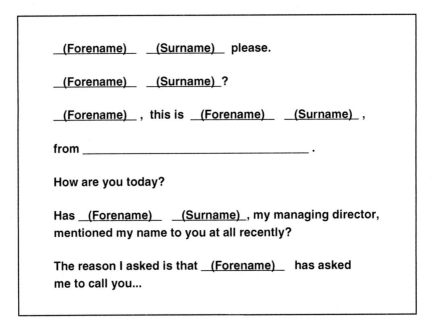

Alternative: use the name of the Customer who gave you the Referral, rather than the name of your Managing Director.

Other ways of making appointments

Another tried and tested method of getting appointments which I can vouch for personally is the postcard method.

Create a company postcard (similar to an ordinary picture postcard but with company details or information on the back instead of a picture), and send it to the person you want to meet with the following simple script:

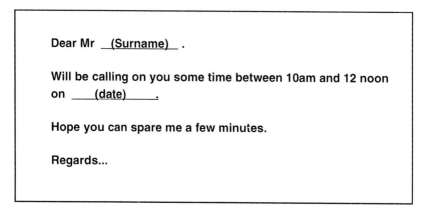

Dear Mr (Surname) .

Will be calling on you some time between 10am and 12 noon on   (date)   .

Hope you can spare me a few minutes.

Regards...

If you feel a slightly more formal approach would be appropriate write a letter with the same message (but not in shorthand – say 'I will be calling...' and 'I hope you can spare...').

Another variation is to send this message by email.

The advantage of the postcard is that this gives you an opportunity to promote your company and its products at the same time as making the approach.

3

Developing the Sale

The Feel Good Factor

People won't buy ANYTHING unless they feel GOOD about it.

And they need to feel good about FOUR specific things. All four. If they feel good about three and feel bad about the fourth, *THEY WON'T BUY.*

They need to feel good about	**YOU**
They need to feel good about	**THE SOLUTION**
They need to feel good about	**THE PRICE**
And they need to feel good about	**THE SUPPLIER**

What you can do to make the customers feel good about YOU

What are the personal qualities that will make you the salesperson the customers like best?

A professional salesperson needs a wide variety of **abilities**. Most of these abilities can be acquired – through a combination of training and experience.

Qualities, however, are much more personal, come from within and are much more difficult to acquire. They stem from childhood and early education. Some qualities are even generic and hereditary hence that old question – 'Are good salespeople born or are they made?'

Set out below is a list of the top 12 qualities most customers look for in a salesman. There may be other qualities which your own customers look for in a salesman, but each of these qualities is likely to feature high in their list of preferences.

1. A Firm Belief in the Value of the Job

This does not refer to your current job title and position; it refers to the job of Selling in its widest sense.

Some salespeople, maybe because of their technical backgrounds or academic qualifications, resent being expected to actually SELL! But to succeed in Selling, it is vitally important that you have and hold a firm belief in the value of Selling as a profession.

2. Empathy

Empathy is the ability to understand why a person holds a particular point of view without necessarily agreeing with it.

You cannot afford the luxury of dealing only with those customers with whom you agree and therefore sympathise.

3. Acceptability to People

With Empathy, you will be able to accept other people. Whether or not they accept YOU however, is another matter. The job of a salesperson involves close association with people at all levels. It is important that you are accepted in the fullest sense by all these people.

Your appearance has got to be right for the job and for the occasion. You have to behave at all times in a competent way. You must be careful about personal hygiene. You should not, of course, try to assume a false personality; but there is nothing wrong in planning to achieve the personal acceptance of others.

4. Enthusiasm

The last four letters of the word ENTHUSIASM stand for 'I am sold myself'.

There is only one thing in Selling more infectious than Enthusiasm – and that is LACK of Enthusiasm.

You must work up enthusiasm for what you are selling, if you expect any customer to become enthusiastic, and to buy.

5. Self-Confidence

You must have confidence in your own abilities and professionalism. How can your customers have faith that the job will be done properly and delivered on time if you obviously have doubts?

Never bluff, just communicate quiet confidence in your own skills, in your product or service and in your company.

6. Integrity

Complete integrity is essential for all companies and individuals intending to stay in business. Sometimes this brings short-term disadvantages, such as when an order is lost by having to admit that you cannot meet the required delivery date, but this is far better than accepting the order in the hope that the delivery problem will be sorted out later and then alienating the customer forever when the inevitable problem arises.

Professional salespeople are only allowed to tell three lies:

- *'It's my fault.'*
- *'You're right.'*
- *'It's been a pleasure to meet you.'*

Earning a reputation for integrity takes a long time and a lot of determination, but it is the only way to achieve long term success.

7. Resilience

As a professional, you must always deliver top performance when you are dealing with customers, even if you are not feeling on top form, physically or mentally.

Whatever bad days or bad weeks you may have, remember that every customer must be treated as if they were your ONLY customer.

8. A Good Communicator

Being fully understood is a skill you should never underestimate. Likewise being a good listener. Fluent communication, whether face to face, on the telephone or in writing, is one of your greatest weapons.

Within this is the art of asking questions, because Selling isn't just Telling. Understanding is definitely a two-way phenomenon.

9. A Capacity for Effective Hard Work

You must be prepared to work hard. Hard work is inherent in the job.

But hard work by itself is not enough. Your hard work must be Effective. You must work SMART, to achieve your targets with the minimum of effort and time – and therefore minimum cost.

10. Self-Reliance

When you arrive at a customer, you may find the situation is not what you expected. Back in the office, you have colleagues and others to help you. Away from base you are on your own and you need to be able to cope calmly and professionally with the unexpected.

11. An Open and Enquiring Mind

Do not get into the rut of tradition. Just because something has not been done before does not make it wrong.

Always keep an open mind for something new or different. For example, you may see a product application which has not been used before. Providing it is both practical and profitable, it could be a valuable addition for the product's sales story.

But do not let this good kind of open-mindedness overlap into unprofitable areas like 'specials'. Together with your Open and Enquiring Mind you also need a Positive Temperament, so that you can firmly resist unprofitable demands for 'specials' and so that you can control events rather than letting events control you.

Take the initiative, and remain in charge of the situation. No.5, Self-Confidence, is an important link to this Quality.

12. Good Health

Good health and fitness enable your Drive and Energy System to carry you through the toughest bad days and help bolster your Resilience and Self-Confidence.

An unfit salesperson, puffing and blowing in front of a customer, isn't going to impress. A yawn mid-afternoon after a heavy lunch is even worse.

These 12 qualities are the top 12 qualities across the whole spectrum of selling activities. However, there are many more qualities of equal importance in particular selling situations. Consider which other qualities might be of particular value to your customers and plan how you can deliver these qualities.

What you can do to make the Customers feel good about THE SOLUTION

The key to this is Communication. THE CUSTOMER MUST UNDERSTAND.

COMMUNICATING IS LIKE PLAYING CRICKET AS EXPLAINED TO A CHINESE DELEGATION.

You have two sides, one out in the field and one in.

Each man that's in the side that's in goes out, and when he's out he comes in and the next man goes in until he's out.

When they are all out the side that1s out comes in and the side that's been in goes out and tries to get those coming in out.

Sometimes you get men still in and not out.

When both sides have been in and out including the not outs ...

... that's the end of the game!

With acknowledgement to The Marylebone Cricket Club

Samson slew ten thousand Philistines with the jaw bone of an ass. Every day the same number of sales are killed with the same weapon!

What you can do to make the Customers feel good about THE PRICE

We will come back to the issue of price later on (see chapter 8). For the purpose of this chapter, we set out two examples of the way you can present price in a way that will make your customers feel GOOD about the price. The key is always to deliver benefits – to demonstrate that the price is low in comparison with the tangible benefits of your product, easily absorbed, and (if applicable) low in relation to competitors' prices. Above all try to present the purchase as a SAVING.

Example: selling cost savings

Dear Mr..............

<u>*Sand Reclamation*</u>

Our proposals for installing a Sand Reclamation system in your ...foundry are contained in this folder.

As we understand it, your aim is to reduce the costs of buying in furane sand and resin to a workable minimum, and also to cut the costs of dumping old sand to a minimum.

To achieve both these objectives, we recommend that you install one of our 1tons/hour FU-RECLAIM sand reclamation units with certain additional equipment.

From the calculations we have been able to do, we believe you would get full return on the capital invested in   months. This is without considering Corporation Tax savings coming from 100% first year write-down allowances, or Development Grants if they apply to you. Alternatively, if you choose to lease the FU-RECLAIM equipment or finance it on hire purchase over... years, you would be saving money from day one without the equipment penny in real terms. We can, if you wish, introduce you to a number of financial institutions that have regularly helped our customers in the past.

You will see from our prices that we are not the cheapest supplier of sand reclamation equipment. We do not set out to be.

We aim to provide you with a very well-engineered piece of production plant, which will give you the longest possible working life at optimum performance, with the lowest possible maintenance and running costs. It will also be the safest and the quietest sand reclamation system available.

Some idea of the savings on sand, resin, and dumping costs, which you can expect to achieve when you have installed your FU-RECLAIM system, is provided overleaf, followed by the full description, technical specification and prices of the system recommended.

Yours sincerely
John Griffiths
Sales Director

Financial Aspects of Furane
Sand Reclamation using FTL Fu-Reclaim System

Example of savings made by an iron foundry that installed FTL equipment and had previously dumped all old sand and resin.

Foundry using 400 tons per week of furane sand, with an average of 1.4% resin content.

Cost of new sand £10.36 per ton. Cost of resin £720 per ton.

Cost of dumping old sand £3 per ton.

Previous costs per week:

400 tons sand @ £10.36 per ton	*£4,144.00*
1.4% resin = 5.6 tons @ £720 per ton	*£4,032.00*
Sand dumping 405.6 tons @ £3 per ton	*£1,216.80*
Total weekly cost	*£9,392.80*

Total costs per 46 week year   **£432,068.80**

Costs after installing FTL FU-RECLAIM (operating costs of FU-RECLAIM calculated to be £0.60 per ton of sand reclaimed)

Costs per week:

95 x 4 = 380 tons reclaimed sand @ £0.60 per ton	*£228.00*
1% average resin = 4 tons @ £72 per ton	*£2,880.00*
5% new sand make up = 20 tons	
@ £10.36 per ton	*£ 207.20*
5% old sand dumped = 20 tons @ £3 per ton	*£60.00*
	£3,375.20

Total costs per 46 week year   **£155,259.20**

Costs saved per week = £6,017.60
Costs saved per year = £276,809.60

Total price of FTL FU-RECLAIM system in this example was £78,000. This included sand silos, pneumatic transporter units, water-cooling system, tower and pumps, installation and commissioning.

Thus, full return on the capital invested is achieved in 13 weeks.

If the FTL equipment had been lease purchased over 3 years with no initial deposit, the repayments of capital and interest would have been about £700 per week, showing a net weekly saving of more than £5,000.

Example: Selling comparative savings

Here is another standard printed page of financial justification, this time for an electric blow-dry hand-dryer against paper and roller towel competition. The next example shows how to justify the change over from roller or paper towels in a business wash room, to ITR electric blower hand dryers.

Assume 100 people only washing their hands once a day, 5 days per week and 48 weeks a year – that is 100 x 5 x 48 = 24,000 hand dries required per year.

For a Roller Towel
A standard roller is 45 yards long; the pull varies between 7 and 9 inches – let us say 8 inches (0.225 yards) and assume only one pull is used for each dry (you know yourself that many people have two pulls) – that is 200 pulls or dries per roll.

The average cost of a roll is £1.40.

The annual cost is thus (24,000 ÷ 200) x £1.40 = £168.00

For Paper Towels
A standard box of paper towels contains 4,800 and costs now £17.68 per box. People use two or three towels to get dry, but just two towels gives 2,400 dries per box.

The annual cost is thus (24,000 ÷ 2,400) x £17.68 = £176.80

For the ITR Wessex Standard
The ITR Wessex Standard with 45 secs timing gives 80 dries per hour. The total cost per dry, comprising electricity costs plus rental cost of the dryer, is estimated at 0.1445p.

The annual cost is thus 24,000 x £0.001445 = £34.68

For the ITR Wessex Commercial
The ITR Wessex Commercial with 36 secs timing gives 100 dries per hour. The total cost per dry, comprising electricity costs plus rental cost of the dryer, is estimated at 0.1156p.

The annual cost is thus 24,000 x £0.001156 = £27.74

That is an annual saving of a minimum of

Roller Towel	£168.00
Standard	£34.68
Saving	£133.32

Or

Roller Towel	£168.00
Commercial	£27.74
Saving	£140.26

Or

Paper Towels	£176.80
Standard	£34.68
Saving	£142.12

Or

Paper Towels	£176.80
Commercial	£27.74
Saving	£149.06

AND THIS IS ONLY FOR 100 DRIES PER DAY

What can we do to make the customers feel good about THE SUPPLIER

The key to this is TESTIMONIALS.

Customers no longer want to be innovators; at the leading edge of technology; guinea pigs. Customers today want to know who else has bought the product or service and how well and how reliably it is performing.

Client lists and Testimonial Letters are the gold bricks of the NEW MILLENNIUM.

How many good, useable letters from customers are buried in the files, forgotten and never to be seen again?

Dig them out. Send copies (at least 10 of each) to every salesperson. Provide display albums so that they can use the letters professionally. Add at least three customer letters to every Proposal.

How many good, useable letters from customers are there in your salespeople's files, jealously guarded, for their eyes only! Who do they think they are in competition with – their own colleagues? Their own Company? Get hold of those letters and circulate them to EVERY salesperson.

A testimonial letter doesn't have to be written directly to the person using it. Any letter to any person in the Company that says 'We are very pleased with what you have done for us' is effective proof anywhere and the most powerful closing tool you can get.

Set each salesperson a TARGET and make things happen. Each salesperson must secure one new testimonial letter every month. No excuses.

After six months you will have enough letters to build them into a special brochure – **'What the Customers Say'** – about your business. Produce a new brochure with a new set of letters every six months and eclipse your competitors.

4

Establishing Customer Objectives

Before approaching a potential customer, make sure you have established exactly what their objectives are the area to which your product or service relates – and what their criteria are for ordering. You can then make sure that the presentation of benefits described in Chapter 2 is tailored to the particular customer in question.

You can do this by asking outright. 'Can I ask you what your objectives are in purchasing this product?'

Better than this, you can test their interest in a particular benefit you are offering.

Example

S. *'How much time do you spend on the paperwork relating to the goods you have to ship, Mr C?*

C. *'Ooh, it's got to be a couple of hours every day.'*

S. *'If we took it all off your hands and did it all for you, would that be an advantage to you?'*

C. *'Well, of course it would, errr'*

S. *'Okay, can I use the savings of this 2 hours a day as the basis of our proposals – and work out some financial projections on this basis – how much money you'll save per year, for example?'*

C. *'Well, okay. That sounds fair enough.'*

Taking this approach a level further you can present the potential customer with an official 'survey of customer's objectives'. Create a list of 10-12 objectives which you believe your customers apply to your product or service, and ask the target customer to confirm which of the objectives they share.

This approach has two benefits. Firstly, it enables you to identify the basis on which your proposal to the target should be constructed. Secondly it gives you the opportunity to suggest through the survey that you can meet each and every one of the objectives listed (see the Criteria for Ordering Close on page 104).

What a sales opener this is!

> *'I've got a list here of the key things our customers have wanted to achieve with our services/products over the past year. Would you run your eye down the list and see if there is anything on it that YOU want to achieve?'*

Natural curiosity will do the rest. Consider my big three reasons for doing the job this way. When you start your sales presentation with the Customer's Objectives List,

1. You switch the customer on by talking about what HE/SHE wants to do, not about what you want to do.

2. You open the customer's mind to achieving things he/she hasn't even thought about yet.

3. You make it absolutely certain that the customer will want you to quote for the job. And seriously, not just to get rid of you!

Here are three examples, all from real life.

Example 1. Computer Training

CUSTOMER OBJECTIVES These are the objectives most of your customers want to achieve. Which of these would also be YOUR objectives?	Priority Order
INCREASE the flexibility of your computer training so that you can easily cater for upgrades and alterations to the software.	
INCREASE availability of computer training within budgetary requirements.	
INCREASE quality of computer training within budgetary requirements	
IMPROVE productivity of new starters	
IMPROVE the training of staff on new computer systems with minimum disruption.	
REDUCE time away from work for training purposes.	
REDUCE computer training costs by providing effective, self-paced, 'hands-on' training at the work place or in a classroom.	
REDUCE time taken to fully train all staff on a new computer system	
REDUCE time spent by trainers on repetitions 'low-level' training, thus allowing them to spend more on a one-to-one basis	
SAVE time spent in the preparation of computer manuals	
GAIN the capability to train staff on PC packages as well as your own 'bespoke' systems	
Other objectives	

Example 2. Regal Windows

UNIT 3 WYNDHAM ROAD,
HAWKSWORTH TRADING ESTATE,
SWINDON,
WILTS SN2 1EJ
TEL 0793 618138

Our Customers' Objectives

These are the kind of objectives most of our customers say they want to achieve. Which of them match YOUR objectives? Can you prioritise them?

**Priority
order**

INCREASE the value and thus the saleability of your home

INCREASE the overall security of your home, against thieves and vandals which would probably then ...

REDUCE your home insurance premiums

IMPROVE the outside and inside appearance of your home

IMPROVE the comfort you enjoy in your home

REDUCE the loss of expensive heat

REDUCE the noise from traffic and neighbours

REDUCE draughts

REDUCE the condensation you suffer with your existing windows

SAVE a significant proportion of the money you spend on heating your home and maintaining it in pristine condition

IMPROVE extra space to your quality of life

Example 3. Vending Systems

Customer's Objectives These are the objectives most of our customers want to achieve from using our vending systems. Which of them would also be your objectives?	Priority order
INCREASE the range of drinks provided, to include hot, cold and fizzy.	
INCREASE the availability of drinks provided to a full 24 hours a day.	
INCREASE profitability by covering all costs, including rental of equipment, at 5p vend prices for all drinks.	
IMPROVE the quality of drinks provided.	
IMPROVE the general image and acceptability of vending to your workforce.	
REDUCE time spent off the job by providing a speedier drinks service.	
SAVE labour by having a fully automatic drinks vending service which is maintained solely by us.	
GAIN valuable office space currently taken up by more bulky vending equipment and supplies stores.	
GAIN trade union approval by upgrading the hygiene of your drinks vending service to the highest possible level.	
OTHER OBJECTIVES	

Building on the work in Chapter 2, complete the following form to create your own **objectives checklist**.

Customer's Objectives These are the objective most of our customers want to achieve. Which of them would also be **YOUR** objectives?	Priority order
INCREASE	
INCREASE	
INCREASE	
IMPROVE	
IMPROVE	
REDUCE	
REDUCE	
SAVE	
SAVE	
GAIN	
GAIN	
Other Objectives	

Once you have established the customer's objectives, you can take this approach a stage further and represent the objectives as **'criteria for ordering'**. You then present these as follows:

> *'We asked our customers why they buy from us. This is what they said.*

> *How many of these would be on YOUR criteria for ordering list?'*

For your CFO List, you need the things which are clearly your USPs, plus a selection of things where you are just as good as any of your competitors – because when you use your CFO List to back up a proposal, your competitors will not be there. Your key 'unique selling points' (USPs) you use in your main face-to-face presentation, of course.

Now, all you individual Sellers out there – don't wait for your sales manager to call the meeting. Get cracking yourself. The meeting might never happen otherwise, and that's a hell of a lousy reason to stay ignorant

My training company, Licensor of the UK Master Class training method, did the full customer survey of its (at the time) 7000 plus customers. Here is the resultant CFO List, which was introduced as a page in every single one of our training brochures, backing up every single one of the proposals produced by our Licensees.

Why 7000 plus British businesses decided to use John Fenton Training

How many of these Criteria for Ordering are important to YOU?

Results Fast

Customers want to see results from their training investment FAST, from improved performance, attitude, sales and profits. John Fenton Master Classes focus on achieving the fastest possible results via John Fenton's genius to get to the nub of the matter every time.

Minimum Time Off the Job

No-one wants their key people away on a training course for an entire week, losing a whole week's production. Half of the fee goes to pay the hotel and has no training value. John Fenton Master Classes achieve the same performance improvement in ONE DAY that other organisations take three days or more to achieve.

Local Venues, Top Flight Trainers

Meeting growing customers' expectations brought about the John Fenton Training UK Master Class network. Principal trainers, each thoroughly trained by John Fenton, promote and lead Master Classes at regional venues.

Customers are looked after by their local JFT office but can send their delegate to their nearest venue, achieving minimum time off the job.

Customers do this with the confidence of knowing that the standard of training on every Master Class will be equal to those led by John Fenton himself.

Maximum Feel Good Factor

People want to feel good about attending a training course. Open minds, ready to learn, from start to finish. With volunteers, there is never a problem, but people who are 'sent' without the option can arrive with a negative attitude, stay with a closed mind and not learn a thing. John Fenton Master Classes are not training courses, they are MASTER CLASSES. Developed by the man who has led Britain's National Sales Conventions since they began in 1983.

68

Your delegates are VIPS. The Master Class Manuals are top quality. Delegates work with unique on the job selling tools, like the John Fenton Story Board on Professional Tele-Selling, the PPM system on Selling and the SIBMAP Master Plan on Managing the Sales Office.

Sit In and See for Yourself
Notwithstanding the money back guarantee, managers often want to check out the training beforehand. Few training organisations offer this facility. John Fenton Training DOES. The manager can join a Master Class at mid-morning coffee break and sit in until lunchtime, discussing any specific questions over lunch with the Trainer. This facility is available at all venues.

Money Back Guarantee
From a 'no quibble' refund guarantee if the customer is not satisfied. Few training organisations are this confident about their product

Impeccable Track Record
The best people to testify are our customers. Every delegate assessment form is on file; every testimonial letter received from a customer, open for inspection.

Great On-Going Customer Care
Your JFT Trainer will ring regularly to check the progress of each delegate you send to the Master Classes, to provide on-going help and advice for future training needs. John Fenton customers are a large and growing family. Another Feel Good Factor.

Best Return on Your Investment
If anyone with a heart problem had to buy a pacemaker, would they buy at the lowest price? It's the same with training. Few businesses buy training on the basis of lowest price. They're looking for performance improvement, they look for the BEST, because they want their people to BE the best.

CFO lists are highly copiable. You don't have to re-invent the wheel. If anyone else's USP fits your situation – and is *fact,* not fiction – then borrow it and build it into your CFO list.

For this purpose, there follow two more examples of CFO Lists that I have developed for other kinds of suppliers.

Example 1

James Dubois & Co.
Chartered Accountants and Registered Auditor
Lynn wood Road, Epsom, Surrey KT1 4LF

CLIENT REASONS These are some of the reasons most of our clients deal with us:	Your Rating (1-5)
PRICE – We give you real value for money. This means we hardly ever lose a client because of price.	
RELIABILITY – We produce your work when *you* need it.	
QUALITY – Our aim is to give you the best – Total Quality Management for a quality service	
RESPONSE – We're quick and efficient: delays cost you money and cause inconvenience	
PROBLEM SOLVING – We're here to solve your problems.	
COMPETENCE – We get your work right with the minimum disruption to your business.	
PERSONAL SERVICE – Our people are there when you need to talk or meet with them. We're convenient; we all know the clients and we react quickly.	
HELPFUL – When we ask our clients why they deal with us, they say: 'Because we like the people; they know their stuff; they're helpful; they're happy; they try harder'.	
PHILOSOPHY – We put our clients FIRST. We CARE	

Example 2

Powersport International Ltd

CRITERIA FOR ORDERING (CFO)

These are the reasons most of our customers buy from us.
How many of these reasons would feature on YOUR CFO list?

Price	We give the very best value for money
Delivery	We keep our promises
Quality	All our equipment of 'Squaddy Proof'. We don't have BS5750 because since 1975 we've had AQAPS Edition 1, the NATO/MOD Quality Assurance Certification
Service Response	Quick and efficient. No delays which cost you money or inconvenience your customers
Competence	We get your orders right with minimum paperwork
Reliability	We have a fully documented record of product performance which proves longer working life
Running Costs	Lowest possible
Maintenance Costs	Lowest possible
Performance	Maximum possible on a consistent basis
Safety	Our equipment meets all current and proposed CEN safety regulations
Communications	We are easy to do business with. Our people are easy to get hold of when you want to talk to them
Finance	We help you to find the money to buy the best equipment
Philosophy	We put our customers FIRST. WE CARE.

5

Preparing a Proposal

The best Proposals are designed with five sections. These sections must be used in the proper order. They are these:

1. The Customer's Objectives

The Proposal should begin by re-stating the objectives that the customer wishes to achieve. These will have been established during previous sales meetings, recorded carefully (see Chapter 4), and should be listed in priority order – the most important first. Thus, when the prospective customer picks up the Proposal and begins to read it, the first thing he reads after his name, address and introductory paragraph is what he and his business wants to achieve. Whatever he may have been wrapped up in before he began reading, this 'Objectives' first section is guaranteed to make him switch his concentration to the project for which you are presenting the Proposal. So he's in the right frame of mind before he gets into the meat of the matter.

2. Your Recommendations

Having defined the customer's objectives, you then present a condensed picture of the goods or services you are recommending that will achieve these objectives, together with brief outlines of how each objective will be achieved, using the same priority order. For complicated equipment, specification sheets can be added to the Proposal (at the back) and referred to in this section.

3. Summary of Additional Benefits

The principal benefits that this particular customer will derive from what you are proposing to sell him will undoubtedly have been mentioned in section 2. If there are any additional benefits which this customer will enjoy, other than those already mentioned, and providing they are relevant to this particular customer, they should be listed.

When you list them, make sure they are benefits, not features.

4. Financial Justification

This is the most important section. Very few people buy anything unless they can see clearly that the goods or services they are considering will show them an adequate profit; or saving, which ultimately comes to the same thing. They also look for that adequate profit happening in as short a time as they can achieve – the 'pay back' period or amortization of the purchase price.

The majority of salespeople expect their customers to work all this out for themselves. Some of them do. Many of them don't. One thing I know for sure – a salesperson who works it all out *for* the customer, and presents the financial justification in the Proposal, always has a very appreciative customer and is always top in confidence and knowledge when the time comes to close the sale. So these kinds of salespeople usually win hands down.

Financial justification can be written into a Proposal in many different ways, as you will see from the examples later in this chapter. The rule on which way to use is very clear and simple. If the purchase can be financially justified in three different ways, you use all *three ways,* the best first, and you finish by adding the three lots of savings or gains together to produce a final amortization figure, or total profit/savings figure.

5. Your Guarantees and After-Sales Service

Don't leave the guarantee, warranty and after-sales service details to the pale grey small print on the back of the Quotation. It's much more important. In the mind of that prospective customer, it might be the most important factor of all. If anything goes wrong, *he* carries the can, not you. He could even get fired for making a stupid decision and buying what you're proposing. That's maybe not the reality, but it's how they think. So put their minds at rest. Tell the customers how good your guarantees and your service are. How fast your service engineers respond.

And back it all up with some third-party references. Customers who you know will be happy to take a call from one of your prospective customers and will sing your praises loud and clear – because you've asked them if they will do this, well in advance. Every really professional competition beater has at least a dozen such third party references tucked away, ready to use, at all times.

Such a five-section Proposal can be constructed in the form of a letter, or as a series of separate sheets, one for each section, wrapped up in a professional-looking binder. Whichever format you use, the good old legal Quotation document can *still* be added – at the back, after the specification sheets – if your company's legal eagles insist that traditions must be maintained at all costs!

6

Negotiating

There are two types of negotiation;

1. Positional bargaining
Negotiating is usually based on GIVE and TAKE.
(You give and they take!)

2. Adversarial bargaining
Does not discuss 'WORTH'.
Only discusses WHO SHOULD GIVE IN.

It should not be surprising that people who use the adversarial method DIG IN and become entrenched in their POSITION. NOT GOOD!

Always try to negotiate positionally. I set out below a five-step process to negotiation.

Negotiating on the Merits

Step 1. Separate the people from the problem

* Move away from emotions, perceptions.
* Move towards facts, meters, kilograms, quantity, quality, terms, prices. Put yourself in their shoes.
* Understand how they feel and think.
* Do not react to their emotions. Step aside.

- Never say 'but' (as in 'Yes, but...' – they will only hear the 'but' – instead, say, 'It is interesting you feel that. However...'

Step 2. Focus on interests not on positions

- Look for any underlying interests.
- Try to find common areas of interest.
- Conflict in Position: Example:
- Two girls are arguing over one orange.
- They finally agree to cut it in half and have half each. One girl drinks the juice.
- The other girl uses the orange peel for cooking.

Step 3. Develop options

- Define as many variations of options as are practical possibilities.... BEFORE you decide what to do.
- Try to develop the negotiating situation so that BOTH SIDES have a variety of solutions.
- Your list of possible options might include:
  1. Minimum order quantity
  2. Extended contract
  3. Delivery
  4. Spec change
  5. Payment terms
  6. Sliding scale payments
  7. Qty discounts (retrospective)

Step 4. Develop objective criteria

Base your arguments on fair procedures or known and accepted standards, such as:
- Market Value
- Expert Opinion
- Authoritative Surveys
- Recognised Practise
- Accepted Custom

- Technical reports
- Testimonials
- Test results

Step 5. Deal with objections

- Try to close down the alternatives ('If we cannot reach agreement, what will you do?')
- If you meet resistance, deal with it constructively. When people PUSH, there is a natural tendency to PUSH BACK. DON'T. Remember Ju-Jitsu. When somebody PUSHES ... step aside.

  'That's interesting. What basis do you use for that?'
  'Where did that come from?'

- DO NOT OPERATE ON THE BASIS OF TRUST.
- When they say 'It's cheaper from ... ', 'Better', 'Longer', ask 'How much exactly?' 'Where did you get that from?' 'Who told you that?'

7

Closing Time

Now we get to the heart of the matter. If you have followed the steps in the chapters leading up to this point, you have completed the groundwork, set up the deal, and negotiated the basis of an agreement. Now all you have to do is **Close**...

The only reason a salesperson is employed is to get orders. The only logical reason for a meeting between a Buyer and a Seller is to give and receive an order – if not now, at some definable time in the near future.

The only reason a salesperson makes calls on customers and prospective customers is so that they can put themselves in the situation where they are most likely to get an order.

The only reasons a customer or prospective customer grants a salesperson some of their valuable time is because that customer needs something; or because they want to make sure they're keeping up to date with what's available in the market place; or because they're looking to improve on something they are buying now from somewhere else.

So what's the problem?

How come so many salespeople grind to a halt when they get to the most important bit – asking for the order!

How come the very thought of coming straight out and asking for an order puts the fear of God into so many otherwise reasonably competent salespeople?

Statistically, no one has ever been struck by lightning for asking for an order. And the world doesn't beat a path to many people's doors any more! Translation? It means few customers volunteer orders. They expect salespeople to ask for them and if they don't ask, they let the salespeople go away empty-handed and wait for more professional salespeople to come along and pick up the order with minimum effort – just that one extra question – 'Can I have your order?' 'Can we call it a deal?' 'Can we go ahead and deliver?'

Way back in the 1950s, Alfred Tack made a statement: **'If you don't close – you're working for the Competition.'**

This says it all. Imagine finding a good prospect, researching their needs, establishing the carrot, dangling it successfully, getting face to face, asking all the right questions, surveying the situation, preparing and submitting a proposal, carrying out a demonstration, dealing with all the prospect's objections – and then leaving them for a few days to think it over.

Three days later, your competitor calls on the prospect, or their company, by chance, sees your name in the visitors book in reception, gets face to face fast because he correctly guesses the situation, establishes how far you've gone, adds or adjusts a few things, does a swift proposal, and does what you didn't do – asks for the order. The prospect has already thought it over. You did most of the work, but this other salesperson actually asked for the order 'And they're here now, right in my office. Why bother with the first guy. Okay, it's a deal.'

There are two lessons to be learned here:

Lesson 1: Ask for an order on every call

Make this one of your fundamental rules. You'll be amazed how much extra business it gets you. And note, I say 'ask for AN order', not 'ask for THE order'. You might be some way off the big one, but there might be a few odds and ends you can pick up along the way.

'Anything you want to order while I'm here?'

'Are we anywhere near getting you to place the order? Every day's costing you £500 in lost revenue!'

Lesson 2: Watch that visitors' book in reception

Don't fill it in with the whole truth. Make your signature indecipherable and leave out the name of your company. But read it carefully while you're making your entry. Look back a few pages for your competitors. See who they're talking to.

On a final note, before we get into the detailed closing techniques, note that when it comes to closing the sale, there is no substitute for a good **presentation**, based on adequate knowledge and confidence.

   If your presentation has been sound; if you've asked the right questions, dealt with all the customer's doubts and queries, presented the evidence and the proof in a businesslike, professional way – the Close will be easy, will feel right to you, is the only logical way the meeting can end.

Popular closing techniques

There are literally hundreds of different closing approaches, but when it comes down to it, there are only **7** closes you need to know:

- The Order Form close
- The Alternative Choice close
- The Concession close ('If we can...')
- The Summary close ('Let's just recap...')
- The Fear close
- The Verbal Proof Story close
- The 'Ask for it' close

Learn these six techniques, and you will be well on the way to becoming a true Master Closer.

1. The Order Form Close

This is the nearest thing to an automatic close that any retail salesperson can get. It means having the order form out and ready in the clipboard from the moment you enter the store. It also means having a copy of last month's order on the left-hand side of the clipboard and the entire range of products printed on the order form.

The salesperson starts by checking what is in the store's stockroom and then goes to the shelves where his or her company's products are on display. This means that the amount of stock sold since the last visit and the amount left to sell are known quantities. With retailing moving at the speed it does these days, overselling is one of the worst mistakes any salesperson can make.

The salesperson then talks to the store manager and suggests they walk around the store together. While they are doing this (and most managers will agree unless they are particularly busy), the salesperson refers to his or her order forms and to the goods on display, asking questions as they go along.

'How's the new line moving? Is it as good as I said it would be? Great! Same again this month, or would you like to increase it to six cases?'

'Is this line still slow? It's going to pick up, don't worry. We've got an advertising campaign starting next week. It would be a good idea to fill the shelf in preparation. Shall I put you down for two cases?'

'We've got a special offer this month on this line. It will be making a big splash over the next few weeks. Do you think four cases would be enough?'

When the salesperson has been through every relevant line on the order form, plus any new lines which have not previously been discussed with the manager, he or she makes a final check on the form, turns it round to the manager and says:

'Fine, I think we've covered everything. Would you just OK this for me as usual, here at the bottom?'

2. The Alternative Choice Close

This involves presenting with the customer with a choice between alternative ways of doing the deal (to distract them from the choice of whether or not to do the deal in the first place!).

Examples are:

- *'Do you want us to do the commissioning or will your technical people do it?'*

- *'Do you need single-phase or three-phase power supply?'*

- *'Do you prefer the white finish or the satin aluminium?'*

- *'Will you be paying cash or should we send an invoice?'*

- *'Shall we deliver or will you collect?'*

- *'Do you want our Bakery Advisor to handle the flour trials or would you prefer your people to do it?'*

- *'Do you need one delivery or two deliveries each week?'*

- *'Do you prefer the Millers Gold or the Organic Wholemeal?'*

- *'Will you send a cheque on receipt of invoice or would you prefer me to collect the account on my next visit?'*

- *'Do you prefer deliveries on Tuesdays or Thursdays?'*

- *'In view of your increased wholemeal sales, I suggest you take twenty bags this week; or do you think sixteen will be safe?'*

- *'I'm in your area next Tuesday. Shall I call to see you in the morning or do you prefer the afternoon?'*

- *'Do you want our design department to produce the artwork for the Ad, or would you prefer to do it yourself?'*

- *'Do you want to go for full colour or save a bit by sticking to two colour?'*

- *'Do you prefer to be in the back of the book or in the front?'*

- *'Do you prefer a right hand page or a left hand page?'*

- *'Would you prefer facing editorial or run of paper?'*

- *'Do you want to pay now, to get the prepayment discount, or wait until we invoice on publication?'*

3. The Concession Close

This close involves your offer of an apparent concession if they agree to the deal. Normally this type of close will start with the words 'If we can....'
Examples are:

- *'If we can get you delivery a week earlier than normal, can I have your order today?'*

- *'If I can persuade production to paint it your house colour, do we have a deal?'*

- *'If I can shave another 2.5% off the price, can we go ahead?'*

- *'If we can deliver this Thursday can I take your order today?'*

- *'If the flour and improver for the trials are f.o.c., can I take your order today?'*

- *'If we guarantee you the inside back cover, can I take the order today?'*

- *'If we take the entire Ad design off your shoulders and do it our end, will you go for the whole page?'*

4. The Summary Close

You summarise the discussion, taking care to explain that all points have now been dealt with and agreed; you ask for the customer's confirmation, line by line... and there you have it. This is a great technique for forestalling 'I'D LIKE TO THINK ABOUT IT'.

An example of this kind of approach, taking each point in turn, and getting step-by-step confirmation might be as follows:

'Let's just recap on the things we've covered today in our proposals. We've covered the performance of the equipment, and I think you said that you and everyone else were more than happy on this point. Am I correct?'

'Yes.'

'We've covered the question of acceptability to your workforce, and again everyone is happy that the demonstrations were well received and that our operator-training programme will cover all eventualities. Yes?'

'Yes.'

'We've covered the running costs, and I think you agree that they are lower than any of the alternative solutions you've been considering ...' (raise eyebrows at customer)

'Yes.'

'And we've covered the maintenance costs and after-sales servicing aspects to your total satisfaction, have we not?'

'Yes'

'In fact, the cost/benefit analysis for the equipment shows you get total payback inside a year – well within your budget. Have I covered everything?''

'I think so.'

'O.K. Can we go ahead, then? Can you get me an order number so that I can get things moving today?'

Here are two more examples:

> *'We've covered the question of acceptability to your production methods and bakery staff and again everyone is happy that the demonstration was well received and that the back-up service and technical assistance covers your requirements. Yes?'*
>
> *'We've covered the cost effectiveness and I think you agree that the product 'meets the effectiveness and improvements you are seeking ... (raise eyebrows at customer)*
>
> *'Yes.'*
>
> *'Yes'*
>
> *'In fact in terms of efficiencies, consistency and product enhancement, have I covered everything?'*
>
> *'I think so.'*
>
> *'O.K. can we go ahead then? If I can have an order number I can get things moving today.'*

or...

> *'Let's just recap on the things we've covered today. We've covered the quality of the publication and how this matches your corporate image. You said you were happy that it reflected where you want to be in your market place pretty well...' (Raise eyebrows enquiringly at customer. Pause till they say 'Yes'.)*
>
> *'We've covered the circulation and the kind of people it will be read by and the long period over which they'll read it. You were happy that an advertisement designed now would still be totally relevant in three years time. Yes?'*
>
> *'And you're happy with the cost per valid reader, bearing in mind .the long life of the publication?'*
>
> *'We agree that for your business to be in this official guide would stand you in good stead for future Council contracts?'*

'*We've covered our people doing the design of the Ad if your people can't fit it in to their schedule. No worries there?*'

'*In fact, I think that's everything. You've given me the size you'd prefer and the position you'd like. Have I missed anything?*'

'*No, I don't think so.*'

'*Fine. Can we go ahead then? Do you need to give me an order number or can I just write the order up on my pad and get you to okay it?*'

5. The Fear Close

The Fear Close does NOT mean threatening to send the boys round the next day if an order is not forthcoming. It involves suggesting that there will be adverse consequences (usually financial) if the deal is not done today.

Examples are:

- '*We expect a 9% price increase next month, and the way exchange rates are moving, I wouldn't be surprised if this puts prices up another ,6%. I can hold the price we've quoted until the end of this month, I think, but to be absolutely certain, it would be safer to push the green button today. How about it?*'

- '*What would happen if you had a fire before you'd installed all these replacement extinguishers? Tonight, for example? If you decide now, they'll be here this afternoon. Why tempt fate when we're this close?*'

- '*You were saying just now is a good time to launch Joel's Seedbread. After all people are prepared to pay more for something different that offers quality and variety and the trials went well in your bakery. Now is the time to push the button. Shall I get our Bakery Advisor to help you set up initial production?*'

- *'Easter is only five weeks away and I recall you were not satisfied with the quality of your hot cross buns last year. If we don't develop the right recipe soon you will lose sales! I suggest I organise for the Sosoft spiced bun concentrate we discussed last month to be delivered this week so you can start production on this premium product by the weekend. Shall I send four bags to start or will two be sufficient at this stage?'*

- *'You were saying five minutes ago how your two main competitors have been beating you to most of the County Council work this past year. In view of this, don't you think taking a full page Ad in the Official Guide, especially if it was facing the People Page – which most of the Council officials are bound to read – would be a good move towards getting you back in favour. And if you weren't in the Guide and your competitors were, wouldn't that make the situation even worse? This is definitely a case where you need to win hands down – and our design people can certainly make that happen for you. Shall I get them moving on some initial drafts? If you can give me the go-ahead now, I'll be able to guarantee you the best possible position.'*

6. The Verbal Proof Story Close

Here we have a good, true, relevant story, with figures, about someone with whom your prospective customer can identify. It's followed up with an offer to set up a meeting, then reinforced with talk of the kind of money being lost while the customer thinks about it and doesn't act. The finale is an Alternative Choice Close: the meeting or give me the order now!

This is the winning combination for Verbal Proof closing. The chances are that the prospective customer will not take up the offer of a meeting but will be satisfied with the letter and the fact that you were confident enough to offer the meeting.

An example of this is:

90

'I can understand your wanting to spend some time thinking this over. In fact, I had a very similar situation some months ago over at Universal Widgets. They had been using Snook's Oils for years and it took their works manager a long time to decide to switch to us. But since they did, their oil stocks have reduced by a third because of our twenty-four hour delivery service. They've got a much better tool life all round through using our special cutting oils and they reckon that overall they're saving about £2,400 a week.

'Look (produces third-party reference letter), this is what UW's works manager said in a letter to us only last month. Would it help you to decide if I had a word with UW and took you over to talk to your opposite number there? Every week you think about it could be costing your company the same kind of money – £2,400 a week.

'That's nearly £125,000 a year! Or can we get something started today?'

or ...

'I can understand you needing time to consider my proposals. In fact I had a similar situation at Nutters Bakery a few months ago. They were looking for a more cost effective production process and in today's environment needed to make savings without detriment to quality. We set to work on a flour/improver package and developed a formulation using Eurotop Flour and Pulsar Improver which gave benefits of dough tolerance and stability in production whilst using a lower specification flour which in this case saved the bakery around £ 100 a week.

'Another benefit was the use of multi-purpose improver which cut out the need for carrying high stocks of a range of improvers. [Name] was very

91

pleased with the benefits and wrote to us last month (produces third party reference letter). Would it help if you talked to them? I can arrange a meeting. I know you are on friendly terms and not in competition. Every week you think about it is costing you the same kind of money, probably more given the larger business you run. Or, on the basis of the savings you will make exceeding £100 per week, can we get started now?'

or ...

'I can understand your doubts. In fact I had exactly the same situation at Nutters Bakery in Bristol last year, when I was Project Director for the new Bristol and Avon Official Guide. [Name] wanted to attract more new customers into their retail shops as well as have a better chance at the area Council and Schools contracts. It took them a month to decide to advertise.

'Here's the letter they wrote me last month (produces testimonial letter). They're 23% up on retail since the new Guide was published and they've already landed one Schools contract – first time ever.

'Would it help if I fixed for you to talk to [name]? Or, bearing in mind that if you take as long as they did to decide to go ahead, you could well lose out on the best positions, can I write up the order now?'

7. The 'Ask for it' Close

Nobody ever got an order without asking for it. Here is how you do it:

'Are you happy with everything?'
'Er, y-y-yess, I think so.'
'Fine. Can we go ahead then?'
And then, shut up!

Here are some other ways to ask for the order:

- *'May I have your okay to go ahead?'*

- *'Could you give me an order number, please?'*

- *'If we can get them to you by next Monday, can we call it a deal?'*

- *'Yes, we can just make that delivery date, but I'll need your order now. Can we go ahead?'*

- *'Will you want a proforma invoice or should I open an account for you?'*

- *'Can I have your order?'*

Salesmen's favourite closes

In a survey of 1,000 very successful hi-tech salespeople, and 1,000 very successful fcmg salespeople, all were asked what their favourite closing technique was. Here are the results:

Speciality/hi-tech

74% Alternative Choice
9%   Concession
7%   Summary
4%   Fear
3%   Verbal Proof Story
3%   Ask for it

Fast- moving consumer goods

64% Order Form
16% Alternative Choice
8%   Summary
6%   Fear
4%   Concession
2%   Ask for it

Two additional closing tools

1. The Most Powerful Question in Selling

This is a question which you can ask at the beginning of each sale in a number of different ways.

Let's assume that you have done some research and found that a particular company uses widgets, but you haven't been able to establish any more tangible objective than wanting to sell this company some of your widgets. You make contact with their key decision maker, preferably face to face, but by telephone will do, and you say:

> *'Good morning, Mr Jones. As I understand it, your company uses a lot of widgets.' (Pause.) 'My company sells widgets. Very good ones. I'd like to see you using some of ours. Please may I ask you a very direct question?' (Here it comes.)*
>
> *'What do I need to do to get you to buy some of your widgets from us?'*

There are some variations on the same theme, such as:

> *'What do we need to do to get on your list of approved suppliers?'*
>
> Then, whatever is suggested, you can add in some confirmation and commitment before you actually do it:
>
> *'Fair enough. If we can do that, will you place some of your business our way?'*

As you become more proficient at competitive selling, you will find that those three words – *'if we can'* – will unlock more doors than you ever thought possible.

You could also attempt to quantify the business:

*'How much of your business would you be able to move
to us?'*
    'How soon?'
    'What sizes?'

Then, provided you do what is suggested, to the manager's complete
satisfaction, the business will be yours.

Starting with a Close

Why waste time on a long sales talk if you can close the sale
immediately? Obviously you have to start with a few preliminaries,
such as 'How do you do' and 'My name is John Fenton', but you
could then go straight into the **Suppose Test Close**:

*'Suppose you like me... Suppose you like the product...
Suppose the price is acceptable... Suppose you like
everything... Are you ready to buy today?'*

If the answer is 'Yes' or ' I could be', then you know that you have a
serious prospect and you can go for it with all cylinders firing. If the
answer is 'No' or 'I doubt it', you've got some more work to do in
order to bring your prospective customer to the 'ready' state. That
could be easy or it could be hard. Now read on ...

8

Overcoming Price-Conditioning

Many salespeople seem to be obsessed with price, much more so than most customers. Their obsession usually comes out in the form of offering discounts, which can become a drug to some salespeople. Just like drugs, discounts can screw you up.

If you offer 5 per cent discount this time, customers will ask for more next time, and the salesperson will have a hard time talking them out of it.

Prospective customers need to be conditioned about price. They are price-sensitive only as a result of the actions of the sales profession.

People use price to indicate the value of the product. If you are thinking of booking into an hotel for a weekend away but know nothing about the place, you would use the room price as an indication of the value of the product. If a second-hand car salesman welcomes you on to the forecourt with the announcement that this car 'has £200 off the screen price this week', you immediately know that he wants to sell you the car more than you want to buy it. If he is willing to give you that much off, then the chances are that you will ask for a bit more. You have been negatively price-conditioned. If, however, he works at selling the perfect vehicle to you, asking you questions about your needs and stimulating your interest and desire to buy, only talking about price at the end, you are then in a more positive frame of mind towards both him and the car. You have been positively price-conditioned.

If customers say, 'It's too expensive', never argue with them and never agree with them by offering to make a concession. Just ask,

'Relative to what?' Establish the facts they are working with. Are they comparing it to the last time they bought this particular product or service? Are they comparing it to something completely different? Are they comparing it to their available budget or to the prices of the competition or to something they heard in the pub the other night?

Keep price-conditioning in mind all the time you are listening and talking. Prepare customers for the fact that if they want the best solution to their problem, they must expect to pay for it.

Never Knock the Competition

Never run down the competitor's products, but make sure that you know more about them than your customers do. Otherwise they could be running rings around you.

If your customers tell you that a competitor's price is 10 per cent lower than yours but they will do a deal if you can match it, they are telling you something very important. They are saying that they would prefer to buy from you. If they wanted to deal with the competition, they would want you to undercut in order to justify the risk. If they can buy it cheaper, why are they discussing it with you at all? Perhaps the competition can't make the delivery in time or produce sufficient quantities.

The customer has already agreed that they need the product. You now only have to 'sell' them on the extra 10 per cent cost – not a difficult task compared to selling the whole 100 per cent of the product. If they claim that yours is a more expensive product, you must know why that is. Is it because it is more reliable? Does it last longer? Is it made better? Is it easier to use? If they continually harp on about the cost, try asking them if they always buy on price. If the answer is 'Yes', then ask what sort of car they drive. If they admit to driving a Reliant Robin or a Skoda, then you are probably talking to the wrong person, but the chances are that they drive something a bit more expensive because of its comfort, power, reliability, service back-up or whatever.

Justify the Difference

People will always pay more for something if they feel they are getting more for their money, but they won't pay more for an identical product. If customers ask you how much discount you are willing to give, don't answer and don't haggle. Remember that, in the long term, the more you discount the harder it becomes to sell. If customers say they want a discount, never reply by asking how much they are looking for. You would be giving them a licence to knock you down.

The Right Way to Close on a Discount

If customers do ask for a discount, check that they are ready to make a buying decision there and then if the price can be agreed. If you can't do a deal today, don't give a discount. Otherwise they will use your price to shop around. Never give a discount to someone who isn't going to buy from you.

Don't feel you have to go up in 2 5 per cent jumps. Keep an open mind, but don't haggle like a market trader. That would devalue you and your product.

If customers say they can do the deal today, then turn it into a *trade*, not a *gift*. If you give a 10 per cent discount, will they pay cash on delivery? If you give a discount, will they buy a greater volume? If they agree to changes in the after-sales package, then perhaps you can drop the price. If they agree to a longer contract of commitment, then perhaps you can make a concession on the price.

Educate customers to realise that if they want something, they will have to give something. That way you are not devaluing the product.

The Added-Value Close

You can charge higher prices only if you are giving added value, but you have to make sure customers understand that.

Explain about all the things that they will gain by buying from you. You have to demonstrate all the benefits the higher price includes. Be brave enough to look customers in the eye and say:

'Part of what you get for this price is me.'

Then look at the minus side, and give examples of what would be taken away if they decide to buy something cheaper. Make some calculations, such as dividing the cost by the lifespan of the product. Rather than talking about a cost of £1,000, talk about £10 per week for the next two years. Then multiply the savings and gains which your product will offer, making the figure as high as possible. You are looking to make the costs look smaller and the savings look bigger.

You need to have all these figures at your fingertips before you go in for the close, but it will be more effective if you actually work them out in front of the customers, as if for the first time. If they agree the calculations with you as you go along, they will have to agree with the conclusions thrown up.

By adding value to the package you are offering, you minimise you own 'price fight' and weaken customers' price resistance.

The John Ruskin Close

Early on in the sale, ask customers if you can establish whether they believe in buying on price or on value for money. They will almost certainly go for value. Later on in the meeting take a business card out of your pocket with a quote from John Ruskin (1819-1900) on the back and point out that it is over 150 years old. Either give it to the customer or offer to read it out:

'There is hardly anything in the world today that some man cannot make just a little worse and sell just a little cheaper, and the people who buy on price alone are this man's lawful prey.'

John Ruskin
(1819-1900)

As a training consultant I encounter many sales directors who think training at rock-bottom prices is the best money can buy. I use this Ruskin quotation on the back of my business cards and I have never encountered a single person who was happy at the thought of being someone else's lawful prey.

Don't State It, Sell It

When customers ask how much the product costs, remember that you are a salesperson. Don't simply say, '£2,000, plus VAT, plus delivery, etc., etc.' Instead, sell them everything they are going to get for the price. Do all the arithmetic- the adding, subtracting, multiplying and dividing- that we talked about earlier in this chapter. In this way customers will end up being *positively price-conditioned.*

9

Closing with a Clipboard

Every salesperson needs a decent-sized, quality clipboard in order to close a sale. You simply can't close effectively with a little pocket book. You need something professional-looking on which to make your notes, draw your diagrams and keep your benefit lists for instant access.

When you first meet prospective customers, you should begin by swapping business cards. If they don't have one, that might sound a warning bell at the back of your mind. Could it be that they aren't decision makers at all? If they do have a card and they give you one, then you should clip it on your board in front of you, so that you never forget their name and so that you use it more often.

Before you start, ask their permission to take notes. They are unlikely to say 'No' and will be impressed by your professionalism.

Plan the contents of your clipboard to make sure you get everything right. It should have check lists of all the questions you need to ask as well as the benefits which you should be getting across, plus any facts, figures or third-party reference letters which you are likely to need as part of your sales pitch.

The Order Form Close

We have already covered this close in some detail in Chapter 7. 64 per cent of all retail/fcmg salespeople favour it, and it is vital that a clipboard is used throughout.

The Criteria for Ordering Close

The Criteria for Ordering (CFO) Close is the industrial equivalent of the Order Form Close. Just like its retail counterpart, it starts at the very beginning of the sale and runs through to the very end. It forms the basis of the entire presentation and proposal.

Inside your clipboard you will have a pre-printed list of all the major plus points for the product or service and for yourselves as suppliers. A second list specifies what each plus point means for your customer and for you (see sample CFO below).

We saw in chapter 4 how important it is to establish the Customer's objectives and criteria for ordering at an early stage. Now you can use this list to make your bid to close the sale.

So you say to the customer:

> *'Which of these criteria are important to you?'*

If the list has been well thought out, the customer will answer, 'All of them', and by the time you get to the bottom of the list you will have large ticks against each relevant plus point. You then know exactly in which direction to drive your sales presentation. Everything you have to do, to prove and to demonstrate, is on the list, and you will have prepared every answer.

Once it is all done, the list is still there in your clipboard and you are able to refer to it as you move in for the close.

> *'Have we satisfied your criteria for ordering on all the points I've ticked, then?'* you ask.
> *'Er . . . yeess . . . I think so.'*
> *'Fine. Can you give me an order number, then, so that we can get cracking?'*

The Ben Franklin Balance Sheet

When you are up against strong competition the CFO Close becomes an advanced form of the Ben Franklin Balance Sheet. In its simple form this involves taking a plain sheet of paper, drawing a vertical line down the centre and writing two headings – 'for' and 'against' – at the top of each column.

This is a great method for helping poor decision makers to reach a decision. The 'for' list, with your able assistance, should be three times as long as the 'against' list.

When it's a ease of customers being unable to make up their minds between one supplier and another, the columns on your clipboard sheet should be headed with the names of the suppliers under consideration.

Your company's name should always be on the far left.

If you have a CFO list, *your* column should already be completed. Take it out from under the clip in your clipboard and slip it into a clear plastic pocket on the inside cover, so it's on the far left when your clipboard is open.

Your competitors get all the right-hand-sheet space, but with your CFO list on their left, how can they win? You never, never knock your competition; just point out the differences. 'Against' doesn't mean a bitching list.

And by the way, you *always* start with your list and never with the competition's, just in case customers are called away in the middle of your presentation. Imagine leaving them with a list of your competition's plus points only – and in your handwriting.

You can win in two ways. You highlight the plus points of your deal, which are over and above what the competition is offering according to the lists in your clipboard. You can also use these plus points to justify any price difference which is not in your favour. You then apply the 'options lost' technique, and go through your competitor's lists, highlighting what customers *won't* get if they buy from *them*.

'Well, it looks pretty obvious, doesn't it?' you conclude, and then close.

The Options Lost Close

The Options Lost Close is also a powerful tool when you're faced with customers who are telling you they're going to wait a while and think about it- and you know they're going to throw away a chunk of money if they do that. You simply have to write down on your closing clipboard a list of the options they will lose if they don't buy now. Things like:

- The special December campaign discount.
- The price which goes up 8 per cent on 1 January.
- Delivery before Christmas.
- The loss of benefit for the month they're thinking it over.

The longer you can make this list the better. Then you add up all the items, having quantified them all in money terms, and you have a lump sum written down which customers can clearly see is the *cost* of their delaying the decision.

> *'That's a terrible waste of good money while you are worrying for a month or two,'* you point out. *'Wouldn't you rather not have the worry?'*

The Wedding-Cake Close

This is a natural follow-on to a comparison of your check list with an established supplier's. You've already proved that you have the edge and can provide a better all-round quality deal, but you still have to fight against years of entrenched habit.

'It would be unreasonable of me to expect you to give me *all* your widget business, and for you to discard old Snodgrass after all these years,' you say. 'It would be like a guest at a wedding reception eating the whole wedding-cake. I'm not greedy. But how about giving us a *slice* of the wedding-cake – 20 per cent, say, of your widget business? That way you keep Snodgrass happy, you try us out and, with two suppliers, you have second-source insurance, keeping both of us on our toes in the right kind of competitive spirit. You can't lose.'

And as you speak, you draw the wedding cake on your clipboard pad, with a small slice cut out of it. But practise first. Drawing cakes is not as easy as it might look.

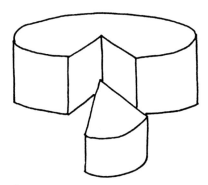

If the customer buys, then of course you go for a bit more of the business each time you call back. From 20 per cent to 50 per cent is an easy jump to make, unless you let someone down.

The Diary Close

Instead of a clipboard use your diary. It could be a pocket diary, but a handsome desk one will be much more effective.

Get into the habit of carrying the diary with you in every selling situation. At the end of the sale, when you have covered everything except *when* the customer is going to get delivery, you get out the diary as you close, open it at the next month and say:

> *'Now, I want to be available for when the unit is delivered. I always like to make sure personally that everyone is happy on the first day. When would you **like** delivery? What's **your** most convenient date and time?'*
> *Most customers will say, 'I'm not too bothered.'*

'OK,' you say. 'If we said, er . . . Tuesday 15 December
at 10.15 in the morning . . . how's that sound?'
'Sounds OK.'
'Great.'
You shut your diary, stand up and extend your hand.
'It's a pleasure having you as a customer.'

Signing-Up Techniques

If you are using an Order Form Close, all you have to do is turn the clipboard round, extend it towards the customer with a pen and say:

'Will you just OK this for me, then? Here at the bottom.'

With other sorts of close, you finish off with the **One-Two Close**:

1. Are you happy with everything?
2. Can we go ahead, then?

Once you have asked these two questions you really do have to shut up and endure the pressure of your own silence – for at least five seconds, and preferably more if the response is slow in coming.

X Marks the Spot

This specific signing-up technique is useful in any kind of selling where you use an order form or credit finance document.

You fill the form out and then you put a pencilled X where the customer has to sign. You then hand the customer the form in your clipboard, which still has the Criteria for Ordering list clearly visible on the left-hand side. You don't need to say anything!

As soon as the form is in front of the customer, get up and check a measurement or something similar (go to the loo, perhaps) and if when you get back the form still isn't signed, offer your pen. If you can bear it, still don't say anything. Words might let the customer off the hook.

The Objectives Checklist

A particularly effective checklist is one which covers the customer's objectives (similar to the **Criteria for Ordering Close**). (See the example below.)

The salesperson can actually use the list to broaden the mind of the prospective customer, opening up a whole new world of possible cost savings and productivity increases.

The list should be produced at an appropriately early stage in the presentation, with the salesperson explaining:

> *'Our products usually enable our customers to achieve seven objectives which are pretty important to them. Most of these involve saving money. I've got the objectives listed on this sheet. Can I just run through them and ask which of them are relevant to your situation?'*

The salesperson runs through the list of objectives with the customer, who will almost certainly be actively worried about some of the items, though others might not have seemed relevant before. In most cases customers will agree that they want to achieve all seven of the objectives; they never want less than four of them.

Once their objectives have been identified, the salesperson goes on to define more precisely what the customer wants to achieve for each section. The precise objectives are written in the spaces provided under each heading.

The seller then asks the prospective customer to put the objectives in order of priority, after which the selling and the justification for the purchase should be plain sailing. The completed Objectives sheet becomes the first page of any resultant proposal.

10

Closing over the Telephone

Most salespeople seem to be terrified of the telephone, but it is in fact their greatest asset. It is one of the most powerful marketing tools available to salespeople, but only if they choose to use it effectively.

More excuses are given for failing to attain objectives via the telephone than in any other area of selling, whether it be appointment making, order taking or closing. Everyone sees the problems involved with the telephone but never the opportunities. It is vital to study your telephone technique in detail, then maximise the strengths and minimise the weaknesses.

Some salespeople seem to forget what the objective of their call is and simply end up having a nice friendly chat to the customer, with no positive outcome. This may be very pleasant, but it is not selling. Others attack every phone call in a high-pressure, results-orientated manner, ignoring the important aspect of selling themselves and not taking into account the emotional impact their voice is having on the customer. The result is that customers don't like what they are hearing and immediately put up barriers.

In between these two extremes is a successful balance of tangible and intangible elements.

The Twin-Track Approach

This can be one of the most effective tele-selling methods. It makes use of two tracks, the tangible and the intangible, to plan and execute calls.

The Intangible Track

1. Make sure you approach the telephone with a positive 'Yes, I can' attitude, because it will come across in your voice and you will infect the listener with your confidence.
2. *Smile* before you pick up the phone. It may sound corny, but it will make a difference to your voice. When the corners of your mouth turn up, your voice *always* comes out happy.
3. Use every opportunity to sell yourself and your company.
4. Seek out the maximum you can do for the customer, not the minimum. That doesn't just mean doing the maximum for the ones who shout the loudest.
5. Make sure that you *never* over-promise or under-deliver. Promises are like babies: they are fun to make, but sometimes very difficult to deliver.
6. Make sure you always sound polite, helpful and caring. Try listening to a recording of yourself to make sure you sound as you think you do. Putting personality and projection into your voice takes constant practice.
7. Remain alert to customers' moods and tones of voice, and then respond accordingly. Listening is a conscious mental process, whereas hearing is just a physical act.
8. Empathise with customers' concerns and needs, which means seeing their point of view without necessarily agreeing with it.
9. Always accept complaints as opportunities to improve your service, never as problems.
10. Ask yourself when a customer last said, 'Thanks for your help and advice.' It should be happening all the time.

112

The Tangible Track

1. Define your objectives, whether it is appointment making, research or making a final close. If you can't achieve your main objective, what will be your fall-back objective?
2. Always have all the relevant paperwork, records and your diary to hand when you call.
3. Make sure you have an effective and flexible word track, with all your key points ready.
4. Work out an effective attention getter to open up the conversation.
5. Prepare your key questions and make sure they are open and not closed. 'Yes' and 'No' answers over the phone are worse than useless.
6. Make sure you have your benefit bank complete and to hand. You are more likely to get an appointment if you talk benefits rather than features.
7. Listen for 'ready' signals, and be prepared to use a trial close the moment you hear one.
8. Prepare recovery routes which will bring you back on track from the objections which are likely to arise.
9. Promise yourself that you will attempt to close every call to the *highest* objective.
10. Keep a record of your conversion of calls to completed objectives, and check that your ratio is improving on a steady curve.

A recent analysis showed that 74 per cent of successful tele-closers use the Alternative Choice Close, just as in face-to-face selling.

At switchboard level the seller can ask:

> *'Would you be able to help me with some information that I need or would you prefer to pass me on to someone who can?'*

At secretary level:

> *'Would it be possible for me to talk to Mr Jones now or would it be better if I called back later this afternoon?'*

At customer level:

> *'If today is inconvenient how about me coming in to see you next Tuesday? Would the morning or the afternoon be better?'*

If you offer customers a choice, they are likely to make one rather than simply say 'No'. By rejecting one of the alternatives they are, by inference, accepting the other.

Trial Closing

When you get a 'ready' signal, you can use a trial close. It is much harder to spot the signals when you aren't face to face, but it can help to ask questions.

> *'Is week fifty important to you for this delivery schedule?'*

And then listen. If the answer is, *'Yes, it is very important, we would have to have it during that week'*, then they are ready to be closed.

If you can tell that the customer is imagining owning the product, then you are practically there.

Customers will also use 'If we . . .' phrases on the phone.

> *'If we decide to go with you, could you install it for us?'*

Don't just answer 'Yes'. Ask another question back:

> *'Absolutely no problem. When would you like us to do the installation?'*

Be aware of changes in tone of voice. A laugh or chuckle suggests the customer is imagining owning the product.

The worst thing customers can say to you is, 'I'm not quite ready yet.' However, if you are prepared with your recovery routes, you can ask what points are still worrying them and go through things once more.

Selling Across

Always help customers obtain a complete package. If they are buying a product from you which needs something else to go with it (such as sand with cement, nails with a hammer), make sure that you can offer it to them somehow.

This is another way to use the twin-track approach. The telephone is an ideal method of adding on another product once the first sale has been made. Customers actually enjoy being sold across, because once they have made the first decision to purchase they are limpatient to get the final result. If they have been sold a bag of cement it is because they want to see the wall built at the bottom of their garden. So they will be keen to buy the bricks and sand, and to hire a cement mixer and whatever other tools they need. And there is nothing as frustrating as buying a new toy for the children, taking it home and unwrapping it, only to find that there are no batteries. Why didn't they sell me some batteries?

Selling Up

This means increasing the value of the sale and again, customers *enjoy* the experience. They will be very frustrated if they buy the first product you suggest, only to find a few months later that there is something else on the market which is just marginally more expensive but does a great deal more for them.

But, if you are going to add value to the sale by moving the customer to a product further up the market, don't do it simply to make a bit more money, because that does not create a win-win situation.

Closing on a Complaint

Angry customers are like balloons full of hot air. They are in a very volatile, potentially explosive state.

You could argue with them and concentrate on winning the argument rather than the sale. This is like sticking a pin in the balloon: you will find that you end up with no balloon and hence no customer.

You could disclaim responsibility, saying that it's not your problem, which is tantamount to just letting go. The air would come rushing out, but you would have no idea where the balloon would go. It might end up in your managing director's office, with the competition, or on a consumer watchdog programme.

As long as the balloon is still inflated there is a chance that the situation can be saved. The best way is to hold on firmly to the balloon, which means taking responsibility and letting the air out gradually, in a controlled way. This means listening to the complaint for as long as the customer wants to talk about it.

Whoever answers the telephone must take possession of the complaint. If it is you, from the moment you answer it is your problem. You *own* it. Once you have asked the questions and empathised with the customer, the air will go out of the balloon. You then say,

'This is what I propose to do about the problem.'

If the customer says, 'Yes, I agree', then you have solved the problem and the sale can be saved. If the customer says, 'No', then you have to do some more questioning and some more listening because there is still some air in the balloon. When you are in full possession of the facts, you can start making suggestions:

'So that will sort out this month's stock holding for you, Mr Jones, and to make sure the same thing doesn't happen again, shall we increase next month's stock holding to 80 per cent of the range? Shall I just add it to the invoice, or would you prefer a separate one?'

If you pick your moment, you can close very successfully on a complaint. If you solve a problem for a customer you will be cementing a relationship, and they will come back to you again the next time they have a problem.

'Following Up Quotation' Closes

To start with, it is better never to send quotations but to send 'proposals' instead. Don't ring up saying, 'Have you received our quote?' You are merely asking for a negative reply. Instead, try saying,

> *'Last week we sent you our proposals for increasing/ improving/reducing/saving/gaining... '*

Don't say, 'Have you had a chance to read it through?' Try saying,

> *'Can you give me the go-ahead? We're all ready at this end.'*

If customers say that they have a few queries or points they're not happy with, don't say: 'Oh, what are they?' That will get you into objection handling by telephone. Instead, say,

> *'Right, I'm back in your area next week. I'll come over and go through them with you. Which day is most convenient for you, Monday or Tuesday?'*

Exploding the Myth

There is a piece of perceived wisdom which says that it is impossible to get big decisions over the phone. Most salespeople and managers believe that it can't be done. But it can, if you believe it can. Adopt a 'Yes, I can' attitude.

Mandy Birtles, not quite 18 and in her first six months as a telesalesperson for DEC-Direct, part of the Digital Computers Group, proved this.

Fresh back from one of my 'Selling by Telephone' courses, she closed an order for £1.2 million over the telephone. She has subsequently closed many more deals this way, because she has been trained to know that it is possible.

Remember the bumble bee?

11

Classic Closes

Here is a mixed bag of the real-life classic closes which have, over the years, served to make their users rich. They can be adapted and used by anyone who has the determination and open-mindedness to be really successful in this great profession called Selling.

When Is an Order Really Lost

This is about an order which was won *after* the customer had placed the same order with a competitor and paid a deposit of £1,800. The product was a piece of metal finishing machinery – a kind of rumbling barrel with knobs on.

Our hero, the salesperson who found that he had lost the order to a competitor, reported this calamity to his sales director. The sale director said,

> '*Hang on a minute. We've got one of these in stock. We could deliver it to them tomorrow. What delivery is the competition offering on this?*'
> '*Six weeks minimum,*' replied the salesperson.
> '*So all is definitely not lost,*' said the sales director.
> '*Come on, let's go and talk to the customer.*'

So they sat down with the customer and worked out the figures, which showed that by saving the six weeks' delay on delivery they could save the customer three times the £1,800 he had paid as a deposit. The works manager who had actually placed the order was very reluctant to let down the company with whom he had made the deal, and didn't believe that his managing director would allow it. So they went to see the managing director and laid all the figures out in front of him. The managing director was also doubtful about doing this to the competing supplier, so the sales director offered a further discount of £1,800 over the first year on the chips that went into the machine, and the deal was done.

The 'Price Is Higher' Close

This is for salespeople with guts and tremendous willpower. They also need to have a top-quality product or service.

It begins when the customer says to the salesperson:

> *'Your price is higher than the other people I've been talking to.'*
>
> *The salesperson nods, says seriously, 'Yes, it is,' and then shuts up.*
>
> *After a few seconds the customer can't stand the silence and says, 'I suppose you'll say that's because yours is better?'*
>
> *And the salesperson nods again, says seriously, 'Yes, it is,' and shuts up again.*
>
> *After a few seconds of this, most customers will sigh, say, 'OK, then' and buy.*

The 'Phone the Boss' Close

This is sometimes called the **Executive Co-Operation Close**.

This time our hero is dealing with a final objection. He *knows* it's a final objection because he's already asked, 'Is this the only thing that's standing in the way of us doing business?' It's only a point on price or delivery that is holding things up, with the customer wanting delivery two days sooner or digging his toes in for a 2.5 per cent discount. The salesperson can't take these sorts of decisions, so he asks the customer if he can use his mobile to call his boss. The customer, of course, says, 'Sure, go ahead.'

The salesperson rings his boss, explains the problem and gives the impression that he is having a hard time defending the customer's position. The boss gives in, apparently reluctantly.

The salesperson looks at the customer, with the phone still to his ear, and says,

'My boss says he'll do it, but only if I can give him an order now. Is that OK?'

Very rarely indeed is it *not* OK. So he tells his boss to go ahead and deliver, and the customer is impressed that the salesperson has pulled out all the stops for him.

The Coffee Percolator Close

There are some up-market retail outlets which use this close very effectively when customers are on the premises.

When they come in, offer them a coffee and make sure that it is so hot that they can't possibly start to drink it for ten minutes. They consequently have to sit there talking to you or look around the stock, and they become *obligated* to buy *something*. You have, after all, extended a gesture of friendship and hospitality towards them.

The same principle also works well on small, under-staffed exhibition stands. One or two people can service a dozen prospective customers while they're waiting for their coffees to cool down to drinking temperature. It can even be a good idea to design the stand to look like a cafe, which will attract tired visitors to sit down for a rest and refreshment.

Public Closes

This means giving a presentation to a group of people, who may not all be from the same company, and closing the whole group. If you can get one or two of them to say 'Yes', the whole group will follow, rather like sheep.

I gave a demonstration of this technique live on television at a time when high unemployment was a 'hot' issue. There was only one chance to get this right. The customers were forty members of the Cheltenham Townswomen's Guild, and the product was the all-British McLoud Dishwasher. It was more expensive than some of the competitors' products but very reliable.

I used three pre-close stages to get to the real close, and all forty prospects said 'Yes'. It went as follows:

Pre-Close 1

> *'How do you feel about unemployment? I read somewhere the other day that we're losing 20,000 jobs a month in our manufacturing industries.*
>
> *'Terrible. But I also read that if everyone in the country spent another £3 a week on British goods instead of foreign goods, this 20,000 jobs a month loss would turn into a 60,000 jobs a month gain. It's staggering to think it could be that easy, isn't it?'*

Pre-Close 2

> *'How do you feel about washing up?' (Muttered replies like 'horrible'.) 'How many hours a week do you spend doing it?' ('Too many.') 'Twenty perhaps? What could you do with that time if you didn't have to waste it washing up? How many of you have a dishwasher?' (Only one.) 'So all the rest of you do it the manual way.'*

Pre-Close 3

'When you go shopping, especially when you're looking for something for the home that has to last a long time, do you look for the cheapest price or the best value for money?' (Unanimous 'best value'.)

The Real Close

*'I would like to demonstrate to you a **British** product that's a bit more expensive than others you could buy, but it's very, very good – and if you like what you see, I'd like to arrange to do **another** demonstration in each of your homes, to make sure you can live happily with a dishwasher. How do you feel about that?'*

(Unanimous 'Yes'.)

The Clive Holmes Cocktail Party Close

This is a classic from the king of the British life insurance industry. Clive Holmes is Life President of the Life Insurance Association, and a life member of the Million Dollar Round Table.

Very early in his career Clive discovered that if you tell a stranger at a cocktail party that you sell life insurance, the stranger disappears, almost like a puff of smoke. The words 'I sell life assurance' can clear a room faster than shouting 'Fire!' Clive went to a lot of cocktail parties because he knew that if he ran out of people to sell to, he was out of business. So he perfected a subtle change in his technique for his cocktail party prospecting which went like this:

Stranger: *What do you do for a living?*

Clive: *I buy life insurance.*

Stranger (puzzled):   *What do you mean, you buy life insurance?*

Clive: *I buy life insurance for people at the lowest possible cost for the maximum possible benefits. Would you like me to buy you some?*

The Victor Hugo Close

This is another particularly good close for the pensions industry, using a quote from Victor Hugo:

> *'Nothing, not even prison bars, can hold a man as securely as poverty in old age.'*

Like THE JOHN Ruskin Close discussed earlier, this is a great quote to have on the back of a business card, and can be adapted to fit most selling situations.

Any salesperson selling something which will increase the customer's profits can use the quote, just adding:

> *'. . . and if your business doesn't increase its profits, you won't have much money to put into your pension fund, will you? Which, as you know, is the most tax-efficient thing a company owner can do with his money, Mr Jones.'*

The Audiocassette Close

This classic is about a salesperson who had submitted a proposal for a significant chunk of business to a customer he already knew reasonably well. But when he came to follow up the proposal, and secure the order, he found that his customer was never there when he telephoned or called in person. It wasn't evasion. The guy really was terribly busy, with responsibilities for three factories, each one fifty or sixty miles from the other. He was spending 80 per cent of his day in his car, and most of the other 20 per cent in the factories. His secretary saw him only for about ten minutes a week.

The salesperson knew that the customer was a Frank Sinatra fan, as he was himself. So he unearthed a very old, very rare 78 record of Sinatra that he was sure the customer didn't have. He copied the track on to a cassette and sent it to the customer through the post, with a suitable covering letter.

A few days later, the customer was in his car, burning up the miles towards one of his factories and playing the tape. After a few minutes of Sinatra, the music faded and he heard instead the salesperson's voice.

> *'Hi, Mr Arnold, I hope you like this tape. Sorry to interrupt, but I've been trying to speak to you for weeks now about our proposals for your chemicals supplies next period. If you have no queries, could you telex us the go ahead. Thanks. Enjoy the music.'*

And the music faded back in again.

The customer was so taken with the originality of the close, he phoned his secretary when he got to his destination and told her to send the telex.

Closing a Closed Tender

There are, of course, many unethical ways to close a closed tender what the Stock Exchange might call insider dealing and the law calls corruption. But there is also a perfectly ethical way of achieving the same end.

Most major closed tender deals take weeks or even months to reach tender stage. During those weeks or months, the suppliers who are being considered have numerous meetings with the customer's technical, commercial and financial people, to gather all the facts and figures so that they can tender meaningfully.

So this is what you do... After every meeting you send a report of the meeting's conclusions to every relevant customer contact. The report highlights the key benefits/cost savings that your deal will give the customer. By the time the tenders are in, there should be a dozen or more such reports in the customer's contact files. All or most of them stand a good chance of being paper-clipped to your tender when it is examined. This is not a guarantee that you will win, but one company which has to give closed tenders regularly wins more than 50 per cent of the business it goes in for in this way and at nowhere near the lowest price.

The 'We've a Van in Your Area Tomorrow' Close

This is an absurdly simple classic which enabled one company in Berkshire to boost its sales turnover by 20 per cent in the first and second years that it started employing the close regularly.

Van deliveries are scheduled for the week ahead. The schedule is passed to someone in the sales office whose task it is to telephone every customer on the schedule the day before the scheduled delivery and say:

> *'You've got a delivery coming from us tomorrow. Is there anything else you'd like us to put on the van for you?'*

Then that person calls up on the computer terminal all the other customers in the same town or on the route the delivery van will be taking and telephones them:

> *'We've a van coming your way tomorrow. Is there anything we can put on it for you?'*

It seems so obvious, doesn't it? But we know from experience that what this company is doing is exceptional. Too many companies have systems which are not flexible enough to *allow* for a fast turnaround, or else their sales offices think it would be too much trouble. Many simply haven't thought about it – or believe it is too simple to bother about. One company executive actually said to me: 'It's not very sophisticated, is it?'

But an increase of 20 per cent in sales is a pretty sophisticated result.

12

Closing a Board of Directors

The boardroom can be a battlefield for salespeople, and in order to win any battle you need confidence. But that is the one thing that can drain out of any salesperson when confronted by a high-powered board of directors.

There are two battles going on in most of these situations, and neither of them is between the salesperson and the customers, because that sort of battle can lead only to a win-lose situation.

The first battle is happening within the salesperson's mind. When you lack confidence it means that there is a conflict going on inside your brain, the rational side fighting with the abstract side. That leads to an increased flow of adrenalin to keep the blood pumping around the body fast, so that you can run away from the problem. Successful salespeople, however, can never run away, not if they want to close the sale, but that doesn't make them any less nervous.

To win the battle of the nerves, you have to face up truthfully to what you are feeling. If you tell yourself you are feeling 'nervous' about the situation, you are actually using a euphemism for 'scared'. You must come to terms with how you feel and then you can deal with it. The way to achieve confidence is simply to know more about the subject than the people who sit around the boardroom table. If you are sure that you know more, your confidence will soar.

The second battle is between the board members themselves. Whenever you have a team of ambitious, intelligent, opinionated people, you will have differences of opinion and conflicts of interest. Some directors will be interested in maintaining the status quo, while others will be intent on changing it. Some will want what you are proposing, while others will be dead set against it. Your proposals are a theatre of war for these people.

At one company a new director was taken into the boardroom for the first time and shown the table. The man showing him around told him about a recently elected Labour politician going into the House of Commons for the first time and sitting down on the benches with the man who was showing him around. Looking across at the other side, the new MP said: 'So, that's the enemy, is it?'

'No, no,' said the old hand, 'that's the Government. This is the enemy here.'

That's the problem which most people face in the average boardroom. To overcome this problem you need to know what is motivating everyone, and to understand some of the basics of human behaviour and personality.

The Behavioural Mix

Everyone is made up of a unique behavioural mix. Personality characteristics are particularly noticeable around any boardroom table. Here are four examples:

The Director with a Strong Need for Domination

This sort of customer tends to be abrasive and defiant in their behaviour. They may brag a lot and drop names more often than is necessary. They will try to monopolise any discussion and will be impatient with other people, interrupting them when they try to argue or put alternative points of view. They are argumentative and probably see no need for salespeople to exist at all. They will always claim to have all the answers.

A typical 'Domination' director once said that he didn't see why his company needed a salesforce; he saw salespeople as being a 'carbuncle on the backside of industry'.

How to deal with 'Domination' Customers

1. Never try to confront them. If you meet aggression with aggression you will just have conflict.
2. Control them passively by using open questions. Give them the impression that they are controlling the meeting.
3. Give them plenty of back-up data because you will need to cross every 't' and dot every 'i'.
4. Let them drive the sale for you.
5. Leave it to the other directors to shut them up.

The Director with a Strong Need for Security

These people work on the premise that they had better keep their mouth shut so that their colleagues won't think they are stupid.

The stance here is silent and defensive. They will shrink back and say little, and will be very reluctant to come to a decision. They hate risk and want to maintain the status quo wherever possible. They are procrastinators and take a 'that won't work' attitude to everything.

One 'Security' director was heard agonising over a decision and saying, 'No, we made a wrong decision on something like this in 1978, and in 1984, and I'm not going to go through it again.'

They were talking about buying a coffee machine.

How to Deal with 'Security' Customers

1. Listen patiently and use open questions. You will need to watch their body language because they won't be saying much.
2. Do progress checks to ensure that you are talking on the same wavelength, and look for ways to become more tuned in to theirs.
3. Make the running with suggestions.
4. Prove that you have a good, reliable track record for both product and company.

The Director with a Strong Need for Popularity

These people want to be liked first and to be effective second. That means they will always be friendly and agree readily with everything you say. It will be only a superficial agreement, however. They roam from topic to topic and they avoid conflict with poor-quality compromises.

A 'Popularity' managing director once said that he had a problem with a particular person in his team who hadn't achieved a single financial target or stuck to the business plan. Instead of firing him, however, he promoted him to 'Head of Special Projects'.

How to deal with 'Popularity' Customers

1. Be positive.
2. Stress optimism.
3. Use closed questions to discourage them from talking too much.
4. Don't focus on this person unless you have to.
5. Use this person as a supporter for your proposals.

The Customer with a Strong Need for Self-Realisation

These people take a pragmatic, flexible approach. They are solution-minded people. They tend to be self-assured but not arrogant. They are usually candid and open and will look for themes. They will not labour points and will take risks if they feel the returns are worth it. They are happy to be proved wrong and see differing opinions as constructive. They like constructive argument. They don't suffer fools gladly and, sadly, they are the customers that most salespersons like least, because they are very demanding and will test salespeople's beliefs. If a salesperson says something to them, they may well look him or her in the eye and say, 'Do you really believe that?' They are looking for conviction not sales-speak.

How to Deal with 'Self-Realisation' Customers

1. Stick to the point.
2. Be factual; don't use sales-speak.
3. Express conviction.
4. Welcome pertinent questions.

The 'Self-Realisation' customer is flexible and pragmatic, and that is precisely the sort of behaviour which good salespeople should adopt. They should be solution-minded and results-orientated.

Success in the boardroom, as in any selling situation, comes from preparation and planning and understanding what makes your customers tick.

How to Control the Meeting

When facing a board of directors, you need to remain in control of the meeting, which means laying plans. The secretary to the managing director or chief executive will always be a key player in these plans. This person takes the minutes, sets out the agenda and keeps in touch with everyone. They are a gold mine of information and make a useful ally. They know who reports to whom and who has responsibilities for different parts of the project, and they will know which director puts the final signature on the order form. The salesperson needs to know which directors have a central interest in the purchase and which have only a marginal interest. This is all information which the secretary can tell you.

Make sure that you have a copy of the agenda and a list of the attendees before the meeting, and find out if the meeting has been called specifically to discuss your proposal and, if not, what its purpose is. Find out how much time you are going to have, and what questions they are likely to ask you. Enquire whether they would like you to take some technical support with you to field difficult questions, and then do all the research you can on the company itself, with annual reports for the previous few years and anything else you can lay your hands on. Build up a profile of each director who will be there, knowing what their job history is, what their particular specialisation is and where they fit into the decision-making unit. Are they there to evaluate or to decide?

Finally, you need to know what competition you are up against and what benefits there are for the directors in saying 'Yes' to your proposition or to another one.

Some decisions taken in a boardroom have only a marginal effect on the customer company, while others have a major effect. So you need to build a benefit bank for each director, relevant to his or her needs. You need to ascertain whether the decision is going to change the balance of power around the table.

Remember, the more research you do, the more control you will have.

Seating

You can win or lose control of the meeting by being in the right or wrong seat. Never sit in the chairman's seat. Look for somewhere neutral to sit, somewhere half-way down the table. Sit as far as possible from the 'Popularity' person, because they have least credibility, and as near as possible to the 'Self-Realisation' person, because they have the most credibility, and you want to gain credibility by association.

Use of Names

The use of names will also help you to gain control. Draw up a seating plan with everyone's name on which you can refer to as you go along. The only reason not to use people's names is because you have forgotten them.

Introduce yourself properly and professionally.

With names you can control the conversation, calling people in or shutting them out. 'OK, Mr Jones,' you can say, 'can I direct this question particularly at you? How many people are currently tied up in this project?'

Flip Charts

Flip chart presentations are another useful way of putting over your message. Make sure the flip chart is set up beforehand, and link it to the seating plan if possible.

Never show what you are going to talk about until you reach the relevant point in the presentation, otherwise you will take away any dramatic impact and give them time to mull over certain points out of context. Have 90 per cent of the chart prepared beforehand, so that your performance is already rehearsed, and 10 per cent to be filled in 'live' to give drama and relevance to the presentation, and to make it personal to the people in the room that day. You can outline lightly in pencil beforehand the things that you going to fill in on the flip chart in front of them.

The Quality Close

Senior decision makers are always interested in justification, so list on your flip chart all the reasons why they should buy from you, tailoring the reasons to each person around the table: the proposals to the production director will show how you will help production; the proposals to the finance director will show how you will cut costs; other directors will be interested in your added-value benefits.

You are selling the 'quality' of your company, its track record and commitment. You use whatever references you can to give these senior decision makers a watertight case for why they should use you.

Closing with Figures

You can achieve great things with figures, so why not use them to make your case . . . on your flip chart. Don't use industry norm figures, averages or mean ratios unless you have to. Try to use the customer's own figures, because then the members of the board can't argue with them.

The best way is to develop the figures during your presentation to the board, as you go along. For example, ask the members of the board how many people are involved, and what the investment is and how many machines and so forth. Build these figures into a clear-cut case for their decision to buy. Work out the payback and the return of investment and cost benefits.

Often you will find that they are astounded because you have done something with their figures which they had never thought of doing before.

If they can't produce the figures you need, then have the industry norms in your bag, just in case. They are much better than no figures at all.

Concentrate on the costs, not the price, and look for angles like release of capital, reduction in wastage, projected production increases and anything which is likely to be a concern of the board.

Remember, numbers not words: you can only read words.

The Big Gun Close

The big gun in this case means a senior member of your management team, rather than a sawn-off shotgun (although there may be times when you feel the latter could be your only hope of closing a particularly stubborn member of the board!).

It might be helpful to take your own managing director along to the board meeting with you. It could help you to control the meeting and might also extend its remit, with the chairman of the customer company deciding he will attend where he might not have bothered had it just been a salesperson making the presentation.

Again, you will be gaining credibility by association. Some salespeople, due to lack of age or experience, find it difficult to sound authoritative to a group of senior people, or even to be granted access to the board meeting.

A salesperson with the support of his or her managing director can ring the customer and say,

> '*I know you don't want me to attend this meeting, but I've mentioned it to my managing director, and he would very much like to attend. I think he's got some cards up his sleeve which I know nothing about.*'

But don't ever let your *ego* take over. Have the confidence to ask for this big-gun help!

Using the Boardroom Mole

The mole isn't exactly a spy feeding you information, but someone around the boardroom table who is your contact. He will probably be a decision influencer rather than a decision maker. You need to develop this person, keep in contact with him and give him all the help you can. He will help you to sell at the meeting which you cannot get invited to yourself.

The best moles are 'Security' customers, the silent ones, because when they say something on your behalf everyone will listen. 'Popularity' people are the worst, because they are always rabbiting on.

If you can't get into the meeting, offer to give up the time to sit in their reception area, or on the end of the phone, in order to answer any questions that might come up. Very often your contact will come out and actually ask you about the competition.

The boardroom mole, therefore, is helping you to give feedback to a meeting when you are not there.

The Long Walk Close

Often the chairman of a board meeting will want to kick the salesperson out of the room as soon as he has finished his presentation, so that the board can talk things over.

Anticipate this by going of your own accord. Once you are sure they have no more questions, volunteer to go to the toilet for a few minutes while they talk things over and tell them you will then be back to answer any questions they might have. They then have to talk about the proposal on the spot and come up with something concrete to ask, or else they have to give you the order.

If you are able to walk out of the room without being stopped, you will more than likely close that sale, but it is a very long walk from the table to the door.

Never turn round to look at them as you go.

13

Making Sure the Customer is *Ready* to be Closed

Successful closing is not just something that ends a sale. It cannot be separated out from successful selling.

In order to maximise the chances of receiving a 'Yes' and minimise the chances of a 'No', you need to create an environment which is conducive to a successful close. This means that from the moment you come into contact with the customer you must start setting the mood. You don't necessarily have to ask for the order the moment you walk in the door, but you do have to start 'conditioning' the customer to say 'Yes' from the word go. You both need to be thinking that a close is likely all the way through the presentation.

There is a principle, called the **Six P Principle**, to follow here.

PROPER PLANNING PREVENTS
PISS POOR PERFORMANCE

You need two basic plans. First, the *strategy*. This is the medium to long-term plan for how to achieve the overall objectives. Strategy is about *tomorrow*. What are the objectives with this customer in developing the account? Second, the *tactics*. This is the short-term plan for HOW to achieve each specific objective. Tactics are about *today*.

Many salespeople can see the wood and the trees (strategy and tactics) individually but fail to see both together. Both plans must be flexible, since they need to be able to grow with the customer. They need to be organic.

Don't Make Assumptions

A common mistake in these early stages is to make assumptions. This is very dangerous. Too many salespeople assume, for instance, that they don't have to plan in order to close.

Some assume that because a customer has agreed to see them, they are automatically going to make a sale, so they go in in a relaxed state of mind, not selling themselves, their company or their products. They are often amazed to find themselves leaving without an order.

Others assume that the customer likes the competition better than them. This defeatist attitude means they are beaten before they start. It is seldom based on any rational thinking and is just a gut-felt inferiority complex.

Some assume that the buying decision can't be made today, so they leave without asking. What evidence do they have for assuming that?

Others assume that the customer has all the information needed for making a buying decision, and consequently don't check for understanding.

If you assume that a sale is not possible, the chances are that the customer will assume the same. Equally, the reverse is true.

The word 'assume' breaks down very symbolically into three:

ASS   U   ME

If you assume, it is an even bet that you're going to make an ASS out of somebody... and it's an odds-on bet that it's going to be YOU.

There are some assumptions, however, that you *should* go in with:

- Today is the day.
- You do offer the best value-for-money package.
- You do stand by everything you say.

If you demonstrate your complete belief in everything that you are saying, the customer will believe you. Inexperienced salespeople sometimes appear surprised when the customer says 'Yes'. This is because they had assumed they would get a 'No'. It should be the other way round, and once it is, the whole emphasis of the meeting will alter.

Getting to the Right Person

To ensure that you are talking to the right person, research is vital. There is nothing worse than getting to the end of a long presentation only to hear:

> *'I'll talk to my boss.'*

Or:

> *'I'll put it forward at the next budget meeting.'*

Or:

> *'The person you should be talking to is in the States at the moment, but if you would like to come back in a month or so...'*

The first thing to do is identify the MAN. This is all about researching the customer's ability to say 'Yes':

M Money: Can they afford the product?
A Authority: Can this person authorise the purchase?
N Need: Do they need/want the product?

If you get the MAN identification right early in the sales call, your chances of successfully closing increase dramatically. The best way of identifying the MAN is simply by *asking*.

> *'So that I don't waste any of your time, are you the right person to talk to for this sort of decision?'*

You can do this at the first visit, but be careful, because customers might lie, not wanting to admit that they are not in authority. So you must give their egos room to breathe. Try putting it another way.

> *'Is there anyone else you would like to involve in our discussions?'*

Or:

> *'Is there anybody else you would like me to invite to the demonstration we are going to mount for you?'*

Or:

> *'Should I send a copy of the figures to anybody else?'*

As a general rule, always try to involve the boss.

On the road to closing a sale you will come across various people.

The Decision Influencers

These are the people who make recommendations but do not actually make the final decisions. They have to be courted. They have to be convinced the product will benefit themselves and their departments and they have to be given a reason to lobby on your behalf. They are susceptible to flattery and should be told how important they are to the decision and how much their input counts.

The Decision Maker

The decision maker is probably the decision influencer's boss and is, as the name suggests, the one who makes the decisions. If you can get to him or her direct, then go for it. Don't, however, ignore the influencers. You might want to go back later with another proposition and it would be difficult if you were to find them antagonistic towards you, blocking your way to the decision maker. If they feel you have slighted them, they will take every opportunity to badmouth your product or service once it is installed and will ensure that you get no repeat orders.

If the influencer agrees to recommend your solution but the decision maker is unavailable, you need to use the **Subject To Close**. For example:

> *'I understand that Mr Smith isn't available today, but just to clarify it in my mind, subject to his approval, are you ready to proceed?'*

When Mr Smith returns the following week, you can use this agreement to pre-close the sale. 'I was with your colleague last week, tying up the loose ends, and he did say to me that, subject to your final approval, he was perfectly happy with the situation.'

In this way you have made the influencer commit himself. He will lose face if he consequently fails to get the solution accepted and you have an impressive third-party reference to use in the meeting with the boss.

Decision-making Unit

When purchasing responsibility is spread over several departments, or involves a number of different people, it is known as a decision-making unit. If this is the case, the salesperson must find out exactly how the unit is constructed. Who has responsibility for which part? Who reports to whom? How does the unit interrelate with the whole company? Does one member have the final decision or veto? What timescales and communication methods are used?

To answer these questions the salesperson will have to instigate some detailed research and undertake some perceptive questioning. This is not easy, but it is very necessary.

The rest of this chapter is a compendium of rules and techniques that will help you bring your customer to that essential 'ready' state.

Ensure Complete Understanding

Never try to baffle prospective customers with technical jargon, or any language which they won't understand. They probably won't be impressed, and they certainly won't make a buying decision unless they are sure they have fully grasped what you are saying.

They may not want to admit that they don't understand, so it is up to you to check that they do. If they don't fully understand the proposal and don't want to admit to the fact, they will not close. They will say something along the lines of:

> *'Fine, well, leave me some literature and I'll give you a call.'*

Remember, you can't close until the prospective customer *completely understands* your proposal, so *check understanding at each stage.*

The Japanese Way

One Japanese computer company (FACOM) produces a sales check list which has made them a winner in every market they tackle. They call it **'Profile of a Sale'** and it lists the eleven key stages a salesperson is required to go through, from the beginning to the end of a potential sale.

Profile of a Sale

1 RESEARCH PROSPECTIVE CUSTOMER
Annual report. Company structure. Cross directorships.

2 ESTABLISH CONTACTS
Plan objectives for each call. Top down or bottom up?

3 MEET DECISION MAKER AND RECOMMENDER

4 ESTABLISH NEEDS AND WANTS WITH DECISION MAKER
Probe for company five-year plans with decision maker What are the company's key business decisions? Who makes these decisions?

5 BASIS OF DECISION
Unique to FACOM? Relevant to decision maker. Written down? Can FACOM satisfy all points? Favourable cost/benefit ratio?

6 FACOM REVIEW
Review Basis of Decision with manager and assess percentage chance of obtaining the order.

7 RESOURCE ALLOCATION FOR SURVEY

8 SURVEY
Review findings with customer's middle management. Have you established all objections?

9 PRESENTATION
Plan and rehearse.

10 PROPOSAL
Document only what you have sold. Does it satisfy all the points in the Basis of Decision? Sense of urgency?

11 CLOSE
Close quickly or find out why not. Have you followed the Profile?

Aim to Achieve a Win-Win Situation

The win-win situation means that the seller wins by selling and the buyer wins by buying. If you give your customer room to win, then he or she will buy from you again. If a sale seems like a victory to the seller at the expense of the buyer, it is an unsatisfactory close, even though the sale was made. If customers are unsure about making the final decision, it means that they are afraid of something. In most cases this is a fear engendered by lack of knowledge. They need to be *made brave enough* to make the decision. That means they need to be reassured and helped over the fear of change.

Watch for the 'Ready' Signals

Timing is vital in closing any sale. How do you decide the right moment to ask for the order? If you get the timing right, your chances of receiving a positive response go up by over 50 per cent.

To help you decide on the right moment, look for 'ready' signals. This might be something buyers say or do which reveals that they are ready. A typical verbal 'ready' signal might be:

'Do you offer the system in other configurations?'

The physical, non-verbal 'ready' signals might be harder to catch and require a reasonable knowledge of body language. Don't rely on just one body gesture but look for clusters of posture changes which demonstrate that the customer's resistance is disappearing and he or she is feeling relaxed and open towards you and your suggestions.

In Figure 1 below a salesperson is selling to a customer who is seated behind his desk. The salesperson is painting pictures and emphasising key points with his hands. He seeks to transmit his enthusiasm for what he is selling to the customer. Such enthusiasm is infectious. (In fact, in selling there is only one thing *more* infectious and that is *LACK* of enthusiasm.) The customer's fingers are pressed together at the tips, in a pyramid. This tells the salesperson that his proposals are being critically appraised but there are still some doubts. The customer is leaning back in his chair. If he were to change his position, stop pyramiding with his hands and lean forward towards the salesperson, he would be indicating that his appraisal was finished and he was ready. If, on the other hand, his pyramiding were to change to folded arms across his chest and he remained leaning *back* in his chair, the body language signal would be negative. He would probably, but not definitely, have decided 'No'.

Figure 1

Illustrated in Figure 2 below are three different reactions of a senior executive listening to a sales presentation. On the left he is pyramiding again, which means critical appraisal. A sure 'ready' signal is when his fingers entwine and his hands comfortably clasp his lower stomach, arms at rest, as in the centre. He has decided. Ask the right closing question and he will uncross his legs and lean forward, as on the right. He is ready to *buy*.

Figure 2

The next figure, Figure 3, shows three stages of positive evaluation. On the left the customer, seated behind his desk, is doubtful. His doubt is signified by the hand which strokes his chin and by the arm that is defensively guarding his chest. He is leaning back. As the salesperson talks, something hits a hot button. The customer stops stroking his chin. His head tilts to one side, resting on a vertical finger and on the hand that was stroking his chin. He still leans back and he still presents the defensive arm barrier, but he is interested. If the salesperson sees that he or she has hit the hot button and runs with it, the customer's interest may build. He may lean forward, chin still held in his hand, one elbow on the desk. His defensive arm barrier drops to the surface of the desk. *Ready*, steady, go for it.

Figure 3

Now look at Figure 4. Here, on the left, is a very uninterested, unresponsive junior decision influencer. He sees changes and that means more work for him if he goes along with the salesperson's proposals. He is limp. There are no tangible defensive barriers, but anyone can see that he is negative.

Figure 4

How can the salesperson stimulate him into positive action? Perhaps play on the kudos of having brought about a significant technological improvement for his company, something that outweighs the hassle of extra work? A hot button again, and this time we know the signal is green because the leg is lifted into a figure-four position and the chin comes up. The head tilts slightly to one side. Continue to develop this hot button and the decision influencer will require more information with which to sell your proposals on to his bosses. The leg comes down and his stance is wide open, receptive. He leans forward and his hands do the rest, almost begging.

Figure 5 shows a more aggressively negative decision influencer. His arms are tightly folded, his chin is down, his legs are stiff and his ankles are locked together. He is decidedly frosty. But hit a hot button and his chin will come up, his legs will pull back. He is more open but the ankles are still crossed, the arms still folded. Keep going and one arm will unfold and begin stroking his chin – a sure sign that he is interested. Stroking stops, head tilts to one side and he is ready to proceed. Go for it.

Figure 5

Figure 6 shows is a senior executive in the final throes of deciding to buy – he is leaning forward, eager. He stops stroking his chin and looks directly at the salesperson. Don't miss this one. He's waiting for you to ask for the order.

Figure 6

And for any dumb salespeople who have come this far and still feel that dreaded fear of having to ask creeping nearer… if you see this kind of impatient eagerness – palms of his hands rubbing up and down his thighs – ask for the order quickly but confidently.

> *'Can we call it a deal, then?'*
> *'Will you sign up with us?'*
> *'Can I have your order today?'*
> *'How many do you want to stock for the first month?'*

If you *don't* ask, this guy will throw you out on your ear.

When you ask for the close

When you ask the final Closing question, you may well find yourself in a very QUIET room. Silence reigns while the Customer carries out a final MENTAL evaluation. 'Should we go ahead? Have I got any reason to stall? Is this the best deal we are likely to be offered?' thoughts like these grind around the Customer's mind for quite a few seconds before the silence is broken with a 'Yes, okay then', or a 'No, not quite yet'.

You know the basic fundamental rule:

WHEN YOU ASK A CLOSING QUESTION ... SHUT UP.

Say anything else and you lose.

But the PRESSURE you get from the silence can be unbearable. And every second feels like a minute.

If you can't stand the silence and you HAVE to open your mouth before the Customer does ... **DONT LET THE CUSTOMER OFF THE HOOK.**

There is only one thing you can say ... you **ASK THE CLOSING QUESTION AGAIN.**

But better than this, if the pressure gets to you ... use your understanding of Body Language at Closing Time to reduce the pressure.

Watch the Customer's Body Language, focus on it, and the pressure of silence will diminish.

You can SEE a YES or a NO, literally seconds before it appears out of the Customer's mouth.

14

Becoming a Master Closer

If you have developed some engrained bad habits which prevent you from confidently exploiting the techniques outlined earlier in this book, never fear. Help is at hand.

Most of your negative bad habits are in your Sub-Conscious Mind because you've self-talked them so often they've changed from ACTS into HABITS. It is, then, perfectly logical that if you were to construct for yourself a POSITIVE piece of self-talk on the same subject, you could feed it into your Sub-Conscious just by self-talking the Positive piece often enough to turn IT from an Act into a GOOD Habit.

This is the very crux of NLP (Neuro Linguistic Programming).

For example, if your specific negative is 'Nothing ever happens to me. Life is so boring' you could write a PRS (Positive Re-Programming Statement) which says 'I can make things happen' and use it as if you were writing lines at school, until it has become a GOOD habit in Your Sub-Conscious Mind .

Good starters for a PRS

- I can ... I will ..
- I'm going to succeed with ... I'm lucky because ...
- This is for me ...
- It's easy ...
- Yes I can.

A PRS should be ...

- Positive
- Progressive (into the future) Brief
- Simple words
- On only ONE topic

A PRS should be repeat, repeat, repeated ...
- At least ten times a day
- Every day
- For three weeks

The Inner Game

Success, happiness and achievement is a state of mind!

The only difference between a person who's got it together and someone who hasn't is what goes on in their head.

What happens in someone's physical world is simply a manifestation of the thoughts, attitudes and expectations of their inner world. After all, everything that you see about you which is man-made began as a thought in someone's mind.

The reason that so many people don't get what they want from life is because they don't yet realise that all change and progress, both positive and negative, starts on the inside – in their mind – and works its way out into their physical world.

If we are to be successful in the outer game we must first learn the rules to play **the inner game**.

In order to expand on this most crucial fact we must first understand the workings of our conscious and subconscious minds.

Your conscious mind is responsible for your current reality, your awareness of immediate events – the information you're absorbing now. When we try to do something with our conscious minds we call it 'thinking' and 'will power'.

The subconscious mind is a very different animal. Unlike the conscious mind which can only deal with one thought at a time, (did you ever try to listen to two conversations at once?) the subconscious runs any number of processes simultaneously. It contains our beliefs, values and our self concept – the software that makes us behave the way we do. It's our subconscious which drives us.

Part of our 'thinking' is our imagination. Imagination isn't just for kids, it's a very real part of us and to empower ourselves we must understand it and make it work for us. Because what you imagine, in terms' of your inner dialogue, mental pictures, emotions and feelings is taken on board as fact by your subconscious, and because your subconscious will always triumph over your conscious will power, it then sets about bringing imagination into reality. Obeying the law of 'what you see is what you get'.

Your subconscious empowers you, at a subtle level, to do the things necessary to bring your imagination into reality, often against your conscious will. The key to personal empowerment is therefore learning to use your imagination to programme your subconscious mind.

Parking Places A'Plenty

So let's give you some proof. Just try this. Next time you're going out in the car and you'll need a parking space, imagine you'll find the space you want!

Don't let your thinking, conscious mind interfere by rationalising why you won't and how hard it is. Just relax and see yourself driving to where you want to go and there is a space for you. Use all your senses – see the space, tell yourself in the present tense that this is happening for you and feel the excitement of it happening. Just do it. I promise you it works! Let me explain why.

Because in your subconscious, based on your past experiences, parking spaces are as rare as rocking horse manure, you condemn yourself to maintain the status quo and not find one.

When you show your subconscious what you want by using your imagination to give it a clear picture of how things are to be without questioning how, you start a powerful process. What happens is that you engage your creative subconscious – the part of you which gives you ideas and inspiration.

A number of things happen. Firstly you find yourself driving down the street that most people have written off for parking and even if you don't see the space a first, at a level below your awareness you hear an engine starting up, you see reversing lights flash on, you see a puff of exhaust. The things your creative subconscious is looking for that lets you know a space is becoming available – then you become aware!

That's how we work. See what you want (not what you don't want) and don't question how. Allow your creative subconscious to go to work for you.

Once you've proved this out for yourself, go a few steps further. In understanding how this works, start to imagine your life the way you'd like it to be. Don't question how – this serves only to limit your options and shut out your creative subconscious. If you use this process on a daily basis, I promise you can bring the things into your life that you once thought were out of reach. By using your imagination to clearly programme your subconscious as to how things are to be, you're able to influence situations which are well outside your current conscious realms of possibility. Don't ask how; just see the end result.

Our conscious mind

- Our 'thinking' mind. Our 'willpower'.
- The tip of the mental iceberg.
- Input/output device to the subconscious mind/mainframe computer.
- Linear – can only deal with one thought at a time.
- Analytical – decides yes/no, right/wrong, true/false.

Our subconscious mind

- The part of the iceberg under the water.
- Our mainframe computer.
- Multi-processing. Can and does run any amount of processes simultaneously. Still runs while you sleep.
- Reactive – does not evaluate, simply reacts in accordance with the information supplied.
- Does not understand negative requests – try not to think of a pink rhinoceros.
- The subconscious database is more powerful than the conscious mind by a probable factor of 10,000,000 to 1.
- Deals with repetitions of learned behaviour.
- Stores every experience you've had as a memory.
- When we 'try', our conscious and subconscious minds have different pictures.
- To create meaningful and lasting change, we must change at the subconscious level.
- When our conscious and subconscious minds conflict, our subconscious mind will always win.
- Our subconscious mind stores all of our self-concepts, beliefs, values etc. Many of which we're not aware of but which drive us anyway.
- Our subconscious cannot distinguish between what is imagined and what is real.

Our self-image

Our self-image, sometimes known as our inner mirror, is how we see ourselves, what sort of person we see ourselves to be.

Our self image is a combination of all the thoughts, experiences, concepts, ideas and events that have happened to us through our lives and which form a composite picture of the person we see ourselves to be.

Our self image is made up of hundreds of self-concepts. We have a self-concept of what sort of manager, what sort of communicator or negotiator we are. We have self concepts about our skills in DIY, gardening and car mechanics and we have self-concepts about our physical appearance, how likeable we are and how sociable we are. We have a self-concept for everything we are and do.

Each self-concept is the governing factor on our performance in that area because we always perform in a manner consistent with that self-concept.

Our self-concept therefore precedes and predicts our performance and we can almost never perform in a manner contrary to that basic self-concept and even if we do, our subconscious – whose job it is to maintain sanity by ensuring that we always act in a manner consistent with our self-concepts and self image – will ensure that we return to the level of performance that agrees with our self-concept.

Let me give you an example:

Someone is playing golf. Their self-concept as a golfer is average or below and they expect to get round the course OK but they might lose a few balls and make a few embarrassing shots in the process .. '

On the third tee they hit the ball perfectly and it flies up the fairway like a shot from a cannon. 'Fantastic' they say, '1 don't usually play shots like those'. Their next shot is equally good, the ball flies high into the air and drops onto the green. 'Can I do this?' they say to themselves, 'a shoot-out in three?' With their goal in sight they put the ball straight into the hole.

The golfer is now a very happy and excited person because they have far exceeded themselves as a golfer and thus their expectations. They walk quickly with great excitement and self-amazement to the next tee wondering if they could do this again. But alas no! Their next shot is a disappointment and they return to their previous form.

What has happened to them and countless other people in comparable situations is that because their performance has surpassed and therefore conflicted with their self-concept as a golfer, they have become excited and disbelieving of their achievement. Their subconscious has brought their performance back in line with their self-concept. The role of the subconscious mind is to ensure that we always perform in a manner consistent with our self-concepts and self-image.

Had their self-concepts been higher and had they not become excited the story would have been different.

So because our self-concepts and self-image govern our performance in that area, then we must change our inner picture if we are to change our external performance.

Self-Talk

Our subconscious listens to everything we say and acts blindly upon the information it receives.

If we tell ourselves we have a bad memory for names then we disempower that part of our mind which remembers names. So long as we keep saying this then we forget names .

All day long we are not only speaking to other people, we are in regular communication with ourselves.

It's estimated that we have some 50,000 thoughts per day. Our subconscious records each one.

If we say things to ourselves such as 'I'm no good at this', 'I can't do that', 'this will be awful' we are instructing our subconscious to make it so for us.

If we do well at something and then announce 'that was lucky' we are making sure we won't do it again.

Conversely when we use positive self-talk to encourage, support and praise ourselves we build our self-image. This in turn creates a self-fulfilling prophecy.

If we are to grow and develop, we must become responsible for maintaining a positive self-talk.

$$15$$

Moving On to the Next Sale

Getting Referrals

FISHING is by far the most popular participative sport in the UK. Over 4 Million practising fisherpeople.

For a salesperson, FISHING is a MUST. It is the only way to find new customers without spending time or money. It is also the BEST way and the EASIEST way.

It's the BEST way because your existing customers make the introduction for you.

There are many ways of asking for referrals, but all of them come down to the same basic question:

> *'By the way, do you know anyone else who might be able to use our products and fast service?'*

Using your mobile phone

By far the BEST hi-tech method of maximising calls and minimising travelling time in any urban area has been made possible by the mobile phone.

The field salesperson drives in the company car (which is still required for all the non-urban areas) to a hotel on the outskirts of the day's urban area.' Parking the car safely in the hotel car park, the salesperson (it is too early for the first call) has breakfast in the hotel restaurant and, five minutes before the departure time, they use their mobile phone to summon the first taxi of the day.

Their company has negotiated running monthly accounts with selected taxi firms in each urban area. 'Brown wrappers', not London cabs.

Five minutes after the first tele-call summons, the salesperson walks out of the hotel and into the taxi. During the drive to the first call, they do business with their mobile phone.

Five minutes before they are due to depart the first call, they say to their customer, 'Would you mind if I used my mobile phone to ring for my driver? They are about five minutes away.' The customer thinks 'Driver?' and the salesperson goes soaring up in perceived value and status.

Five minutes later, the salesperson is into the second taxi of the day, probably a different one, and on their way to the second call, again doing business on the mobile phone during the journey.

And so on through the day, till the last taxi takes the salesperson back to the hotel for a leisurely cup of tea, over which they do the paperwork, prior to driving home AFTER the main bulk of the traffic has passed by.

Believe it – this IS the lowest cost, maximum business way of doing the business. Swallow hard and try it for yourself.

Mobile phones in general are an absolute MUST. No field selling force can do effective business without them in today's traffic gridlock conditions.

One customer lost because they were kept waiting an hour because your salesperson is stuck in a jam with no way of communicating with anyone, that is probably ten times the cost of the mobile phone.

And EVERY CALL is monitored by printout. Nobody can fiddle these.

Converting your card-carrying troops

Suggestion for back of your Business Card. This example is for a Profit Improvement Programme.

WHICH OF THESE OBJECTIVES BE WOULD
YOUR No.1 PRIORITY?

Reducing your Debtor Days by 30%
Increase your Sales 20%
Increase your Profits 100%
Halving the Discounts you give away
Finding another 20% of Working Time

You are attending a business breakfast meeting. Circulating, you encounter a person you haven't met before.

'Hello' you say 'My name is John Fenton. What's yours?'

They respond.

You then ask, 'What do you do?'

They respond.

Now you know their job, their title, their company ... and with another couple of questions you have turned them from a casual acquaintance into a business prospect. You stop talking and take a sip of your drink.

They reply 'So what do you do?'

You pull your business card out of your top pocket and hand it to them. 'This is one thing I do. This is based on a survey of our customers. What would be your No.1 Priority?'

And you are now into your FIVE GOLDEN QUESTIONS.

On the negative side; if they turn out to be useless you simply say 'Well, have a good meeting', and you move on to another suspect.

How to end every call

What else is there to say about closing the sale?

You've won the order, the piece of paper is signed and in your bag. You are safe – or could you still mess it up?

Alternatively, could you actually achieve even more success from the situation? Could you turn this one successful order into three more?

There are a number of strict 'don'ts' in this post-close situation:

- Don't accept a cup of tea or coffee
- Don't keep talking about the deal – in case you talk yourself back out of it
- Don't drop your guard
- Don't talk about politics, women, religion, the weather, money, sport, cars, other people, your competitors or their competitors

So what on earth do you talk about?

If customers are pushed for time, take advantage of the fact. Be concerned for them and leave – fast.

If, however, customers are obviously not pushed for time, if they are relaxed and happy now that the big decision has been taken and all their anxieties have disappeared, then you can go fishing.

First you must bait your hook.

'Before I go', you say casually, 'I wonder if you'd do me a great favour? One of my ever-present tasks is finding people who could use this kind of equipment (or service). Do you know anyone else who might have a need?

Or you could start fishing by asking:

'If you and I swapped jobs tomorrow, who'd be the first person you'd call on?'

166

Everybody likes to be helpful and to tell other people how they would do their job, so all you have to do is take out five blank customer record cards from your briefcase, a pen from your pocket and get yourself poised to write.

As the customer spouts names, write them down, checking that you get the spellings right wherever possible, or at least enough information so that you can look them up in the phone book when you get back to the office. Try to get job titles and as much information about the sort of equipment or services these people are using at the moment.

You might get only one or two names before the customer either dries up or seems to lose interest in the game. Obviously you can't push people any further than they want to go. You could try one more question, such as:

'Has anyone you know gained promotion recently, gone up in the world or taken on new responsibilities?'

Or:

'Are you a member of any trade association or professional body?'

If the answer to the last question is 'Yes', then see if they can remember meeting anyone who might be interested in your products. You might ask them about their hobbies, and if, say, they play golf, whether they have met anyone down at the club recently who might be a potential customer.

If you approach this fishing technique correctly, you should be able to fill at least three cards, but ensure that you bring out five, because otherwise you'll never complete three. Why? Because very few customers will stop helping you until they have completed half your cards. It's a kind of mental compromise. And half-way to five is three. If you used three cards, most times you'd get only two of them filled in. But don't stop at three. Quite often you can get all five, sometimes even more. So have some spares in your briefcase.

167

Before your first card is fully completed you need the prospective customer's telephone number. Your existing customer may take a diary out of their jacket pocket to give you this. If so, watch what happens to the diary after you've been given the number. If it stays on the desk, the chances are you might be able to get some more names.

Finally, lay the cards out on the table and look at them. Select the one you feel is the best prospect. Pick it up.

> *'Er, you said you knew George Riley, well ...'*
> *'Yes?'*
> *'I couldn't ask you an enormous favour, could I? Would you give them a ring yourself for me, and ask if they have got time to see me today while I'm in the area. You know how hard it is to make contact stone cold.'*

If you do it right, and it does take practice, most of the customers will make the phone calls for you as well. After they've put the phone down on the second, you could say, 'Buy you a good lunch if you ring the other three.'

If business results from any of these calls, you go back and tell your customer, thank them properly and then in three months' time you might be able to go back for more names. If you master the fishing technique, you stand a chance of making three more successful sales from everyone you make.

And you can even turn an unsuccessful close into several successful ones. If a customer gives you the 'I'd like to think about it' line, then you should be able to apply what is undoubtedly one of the greatest closes ever developed.

There is a replacement-window and patio doors company in the Midlands which is well known for its quality and service. Here this great close is known as:

The You're Pulling My Leg Close

The company's salespeople go through their usual presentation, complete with samples, third-party references, photographs, measurements and price calculations. If the customer still can't make up their mind, the salesperson gives a sigh of resignation and says:

> *'OK, but it would be a great deal for you and your wife. The value of the house would increase a lot more than the windows are going to cost. Anyway, I've done my best. Is there any chance you could help me before I go?'*

Prospective customers relax. They feel they have been let off the hook now the salesperson has said they are going. They feel sufficiently guilty about messing them around to want to make some sort of amends.

> *'Sure', they say, 'what can I do for you?'*
> *'Do you know of anyone else around here who needs replacement windows, double glazing or patio doors?'*
> *'Well, you could try Mr and Mrs Smith at Number 35. They've been talking about getting a new front door for months ...'*

Before you know it the customer will be chatting away about all sorts of people who are improving their houses. The salesperson should get three or four really good referrals. They make notes, check on names, addresses and needs, and ask if they can use the prospective customer's name as an introduction. Finally, they stop talking, look down at their notes for a few seconds, laugh and look back at the prospective customer.

> *'You're pulling by leg', they tell the customer.*
> *'What do you mean?' the customer replies, puzzled.*

169

'You've got to be pulling my leg. You've given me four good referrals – people you know – and you aren't going to be buying anything yourselves. You've got to be pulling my leg. Come on, what's the real problem? Do you want to go over the finance figures again?'

Eight out of ten will withdraw their stall and will buy!

This technique could work in any selling situation. It is so powerful it is a target achiever on its own.

16

Determining Your Selling Style

In choosing the closing techniques which are going to work best for you, consider what your preferred selling style is, and adapt your portfolio of closing techniques to suit.

One way to do this is to use the following analysis framework, based on on research carried out by Dr Robert Blake and Dr Jane Mouton (see their book, *The Grid for Sales Excellence*, published in 1970,McGraw-Hill for further details)

In Selling, at least two concerns are on the mind of salespeople.

1. **Concern for making the sale**

   The idea of 'concern for making the sale', covers a wide range of considerations – not only the volume of sales achieved, but also the number of calls made, the number of hours worked, the number of orders progressed, the number of new prospects located, and so on.

   Thus, 'concern for' indicates not only the salesperson's actual results, but the nature of their attitudes, thoughts and feelings about how to achieve results. If you have a low concern for getting the order, then you are less likely to take that kind of action which leads to high sales volume 'than if your concern were high.

2. **Concern for the customer**

   Concern for the customer is revealed in various ways. The salesperson may express this concern by offering special services to the customer; by calling frequently and chatting about business or social events in a friendly manner; by genuinely trying to understand the customer's motivations and needs, and in many other ways.

The significant factor is the way in which the salesperson expresses this concern – in behaviour as well as words.

You can categorise your style by grading each concern from 1-9. The following are some examples of the more extreme variations (listing the concern for the sale first and the concern for the customer second):

9/1 THE PRESSURE SELLER

Their main concern is to get the business and the customers' feelings are of secondary importance to their gaining this objective.

They are Achievement orientated, proving themselves through high performance. Their sales approach is forceful and they do most of the talking. They may be happiest selling quick turnover goods in non-repeat markets

1/9 THE CUSTOMER'S FRIEND

They believe that if the customer likes and respects the salesperson and if the product is right then the order will almost certainly follow. They are sensitive to human relationships and primarily motivated by a desire to be liked and to gain approval – and hence avoid rejection.

They are good at servicing regular customers, particularly those they like.

1/1 THE ORDER TAKER

They have little interest in selling, or in the customer. They believe in putting in the minimum of effort in order to achieve the results which their company will regard as adequate. Their aim is survival, and they believe that the buyer must make their own purchasing decision. They may even appear to be quite successful in handling captive accounts where there is a clear need for their product and there is little competition.

5/5 THE METHOD SELLER

Although they do not seek the highest objectives, they will do a sound job by following established methods of selling and administration routines, with a workable mix of concern for the customer and for the sale. They will be competent and reliable in handling new or existing accounts and may be quite self confident when all is going according to plan.

9/9 THE PROBLEM SOLVER

They have developed a complete integration of the two concerns and place great emphasis on determining the customer's needs before applying their knowledge of the product and applications. They will seek out new ideas and listen to all opinions and attitudes which are different from theirs. They have many of the 5/5 characteristics – plus an open and enquiring mind.

To become a true Master Closer, you need to work as close as you can to the 9/9 end of the spectrum – never losing sight of the needs of the customer, but always looking for a way to get that sale.

Over to you...

Index

8/73 Survey, 17, 25

Added-Value Close, 100
Additional benefits, 74
After-Sales Service, 75
Alternative Choice Close, 85,
113
Appointments, making, 47
Ask for it Close, 92
Assumptions, 140
Audiocassette Close, 124

Behavioural mix, 130
Ben Franklin Balance Sheet
Close, 105
Benefit banks, 113, 134
Benefits, 74
Big Gun Close, 136
Boards of directors, 129–38
Body language, 131, 146, 147,
146–53
Business cards, 100, 101, 103,
124, 165

Change, resistance to, 106,
146
Clipboards, 105, 103–9
Clive Holmes Cocktail Party
Close, 123
Closed Tender Close, 125

Closing with Figures, 135
Coffee Percolator Close, 121
Communication, 52
Competition, knowledge of,
98, 105, 119, 133, 137
Complaints, customers', 112,
116
Concession Close, 86
Conditioning for a negative
response, 141
Confidence, 68, 74, 129, 136
Credibility by association,
134, 136
Criteria for ordering (CFO),
68, 61–71
Criteria for Ordering Close,
104, 109
Criteria for ordering list, 108
Customer care, 69
Customer objectives, 61–71,
73, 109

Decision influencers/makers,
142, 147
Diaries, 107, 108, 113
Diary Close, 107
Directors, closing, 129–38
Discounts, 97, 99, 106, 120,
121
Drive, 33

Duke of Edinburgh, 3

Empathy, 50
Energy, 33
Enthusiasm, 51
Ethics of closing, 16
Excuses, 20

FACOM (Japanese computer
    company), 144, 145
Fear Close, 89
Feel good factor, 49
Figures, use of, 100, 103, 119,
    120, 126, 135, 136, 142
Financial justification, 58, 74
Flip charts, 134

Guarantees, 69, 75

Hearing/listening, 112, 116

Ice breakers, 46
Insurance, 64
Integrity, 51

Jargon, 144
John Ruskin Close, 100

Listening/hearing, 112, 116
Long Walk Close, 137

Meeting, controlling, 133
Mobiles, 163
Money Back Guarantee, 69

Names, use of, 134

Negotiation, 77–79
Neuro Linguistic
    Programming, 155

Objectives, customers', 135
One-In-Five Survey, 17
One-Two Close, 108
Opening gambits, 37–47
Options Lost Close, 106
Order Form Close, 83, 103,
    108

Performance, 56, 68, 69, 71
Phone the Boss Close, 120
Planning for a sale, 139
Planning time, 27
Pressure of silence, 108
Price, 55, 56, 65, 97–101
Price Is Higher Close, 120
Price-conditioning, 97
Productivity, 63
Profitability, 65
Proposal, preparing, 73–75
Proposals/quotations, 117
Prospecting, 28
Prospective customers, 73, 75
Public Closes, 122

Quality Close, 135
Questioning techniques, 44
Quotation, 21
Quotations/proposals, 117

Real Close, 123
References, 75
Referrals, 163

Relevant benefits, 74
Research, importance of, 94, 133, 141, 143
Resilience, 52
Ruskin, John, 100, 101

Sales interviews, 30
Sales policy
determining, 26
Self appraisal, 31
Self-confidence, 51
Self-image, 159
Self-Reliance, 53
Self-Talk, 161
Selling across, 115
Selling style, 171–73
Selling up, 115
Service, 65, 70, 75
Signals, 146–53
Signing-up techniques, 108
Six P Principle, 139
Standard printed page, 58
Summary Close, 87
Suppose Test Close, 95
Surveys, 67

Telephone closing, 118, 111–18, 126
Tenders, 125, 126
Testimonials, 60, 69
Third-party references, 75
Track record, 69
Training, 63, 67, 68, 69, 101
Trial Closing, 114
Twin-track approach, 112

Understanding, 144
USP, 70

Verbal Proof Story Close, 90
Victor Hugo Close, 124

Warranties, 75
We've a Van in Your Area Tomorrow Close, 126
Wedding-Cake Close, 106
Win-win situations, 116, 146

X Marks the Spot Close, 108

You're Pulling My Leg Close, 169